LITERARY PUZZLE BOOK

Christmas 2021

Dear Dad,
  I bet you never
imagined there might
be a Ben-Hur sudoku
in existence. See page 53.
Have fun!
    Love,
    Martha

LITERARY PUZZLE BOOK

120 Classic Crosswords, Sudoku, and Other Puzzles for Book Lovers

NEIL SOMERVILLE

Skyhorse Publishing
A Herman Graf Book

*This book is dedicated to Barbara Smith,
a good friend and someone who has also helped
and encouraged many a writer.*

Skyhorse Publishing books may be purchased in bulk at special discounts for
sales promotion, corporate gifts, fund-raising, or educational purposes. Special
editions can also be created to specifications. For details, contact the Special
Sales Department, Skyhorse Publishing, 307 West 36th Street, 11th Floor, New
York, NY 10018 or info@skyhorsepublishing.com.

Skyhorse® and Skyhorse Publishing® are registered trademarks of Skyhorse
Publishing, Inc.®, a Delaware corporation.

Visit our website at www.skyhorsepublishing.com.

10 9 8 7 6 5 4 3 2 1

Library of Congress Cataloging-in-Publication Data is available on file.

Cover designer: Qualcom
Cover illustration: iStockphoto

Print ISBN: 978-1-5107-4623-7
Ebook ISBN: 978-1-5107-4624-4

Printed in China

TABLE OF CONTENTS

INTRODUCTION

According to the French author
La Rochefoucauld:
"The ocean of literature is _____."

- **without limit**
- **a continual surprise**
- **always worth trawling**

Whether to amuse, entertain, excite or inform, books offer so much to so many. They can also be a friend, sometimes an escape, and among their pages are many wonders.

In *The Literary Pocket Puzzle Book* you can glory in books, ponder over the quirks of famous writers, tackle mystery sudokus, coded crosswords, criss crosses and word searches as well as deliberate over the meanings of words such as palimpsest and squib.

There is much here that I hope will delight with literary puzzles to literally puzzle over. The answer to the above is: "The ocean of literature is without limit" and, whether right or wrong, let the puzzling begin.

Have fun.

Neil Somerville

PUZZLES

1

ANAGRAMS: DETECTIVE WRITERS

Unscramble the words to detect the names of writers famed for their detective fiction. Who are they?

1 Or handout larceny

2 Emerging nooses

3 Or manhandled cry

4 Past major tense

5 At a high rise act

2
MYSTERY SUDOKU

Complete the grid so that every row, column, and 3x3 box contains the letters EGIKLNOTU in any order. One row or column contains the seven-letter name of a writer.
Who is it?

		E				U		
	L			K	I			
K		I		O				
		O	G				E	
I			O		N			L
	T				K	G		
				U		E		T
			L	G			O	
		L				N		

3

WORD SEARCH: POETS

```
G A G I N J C E A I K L Y U C Y N
V B A B N O O B S H W E I E U B O
X Y Y V X P S F E L E N E N A S Y
Q H A R V D U Y V L Z P O S N T E
Z E O B O T N G N A L S H T Z T S
C G U B L N W E F N I O X K L Z E
T I O R Z A W R S E E I C E M I A
T R L R V E K A S J F T O J Y I M
V N E D L K M E P R J U C E F N B
S A G A G O D P O P E Z L R I P Y
Z T N N H O L S E T H L W E T U K
M Y A T R R T E W H E D E M K B A
K F Q E Z B V K S H T D L O N R A
W E Q D K T N A S C K E A H V E P
L I G R I V C H N B J N O J G C I
M E P N K G U S S L C P T G V H W
J B K S G O L D S M I T H Z I T Y
```

Ralph Waldo Emerson declared, "Poets are not to be seen."
With the following great names well hidden in the grid,
now is the time to seek them out.

Angelou	Homer
Arnold	Keats
Basho	Milton
Belloc	Noyes
Blake	Poe
Brecht	Pope
Brooke	Shakespeare
Byron	Shelley
Dante	Tennyson
Frost	Thomas
Goethe	Virgil
Goldsmith	Yeats

4
WRITERS' TALK

The following are incomplete quotes from Isaac Asimov, Samuel Beckett, and Matthew Arnold. Complete the quotes with each author's exact words.

1 "The one absolute requirement for me to write . . . is _____."
    a) solitude
    b) to be awake
    c) a deadline

2 "_____ is the main condition of the artistic experience."
    a) Poverty
    b) Loneliness
    c) Suffering

3 "_____ is literature in a hurry."
    a) Journalism
    b) A short story
    c) Drama

5
CRYPTOGRAM

Solve the cryptogram to discover a thought of a celebrated writer. To give you a start, T = B and Y = D.

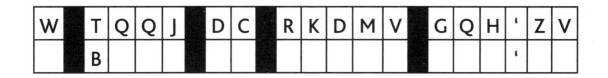

L	K	V		T	V	C	L		L	D	O	V		X	Q	Z		B	M	W	F	F	D	F	I
				B																					

W		T	Q	Q	J		D	C		R	K	D	M	V		G	Q	H	'	Z	V
		B																	'		

Y	Q	D	F	I		L	K	V		Y	D	C	K	V	C.
D										D					.

W	I	W	L	K	W		U	K	Z	D	C	L	D	V

6
ENTITLED

The letters of the title of a well-known book have been numbered one to nine. Solve the clues to discover the title and, once solved, the name of the book's main character.

Letters 7, 5, 9, and 2 give us all of two

Letters 1, 8, 9, 4, and 3 give us a tax

Letters 6, 8, 1, and 3 give us a nibble

Letters 2, 5, and 7 give us part of a cooker

With letters 6, 3, and 9 being a wager.

1	2	3	4	5	6	7	8	9

7

CODED CROSSWORD

Each letter of the alphabet has been replaced by a number. To solve the puzzle, you must decide which letter is represented by which number. To help you start, one word has been partially completed. When you have solved the code, complete the grid at the bottom of the page to reveal a name. Which book did this person inspire?

14				3		15		1		2		26		23
8	16	17	15	2	18	9		2	11	11	9	24	11	2
2		15		10		13		16		1		11		1
4	24	2	1	9	15	12		21	15 R	6 O	13 T	9	18	9
9		22				21		26		20		5		25
11	26	22	2	21	21	9	2	15		2	25	26	17	26
				2				9		20		24		24
26	24	13	9	18	9	15			15	26	11	18	9	22
24		15		9		9				9				
22	7	26	19	13		21	15	26	9	22	13	25	9	12
13		8		8		6		24				9		26
2	11	16	26	15	9	15		15	26	17	20	2	18	9
13		1		24		13		8		6		21		25
9	1	26	25	9	12	9		22	21	6	13	13	9	11
11		15		15		11		3		4				22

1	2	3	4	5	6 O	7	8	9	10	11	12	13 T
14	15 R	16	17	18	19	20	21	22	23	24	25	26

2	25	9	5	2	24	11	9	15		22	9	25	4	26	15	4

8
CROSSED WORDS

Solve the clues correctly and the letters in the shaded squares will spell the name of an influential author.

1 Small cave
2 Safe
3 Small hand tool
4 Come out
5 Promise
6 Find

MINI SUDOKU: EDITOR

Mark Twain wrote, "Only kings, presidents, editors, and people with tapeworms have the right to use the editorial 'we'." And with editors so nobly mentioned and important to many a book, enjoy this mini sudoku by completing the grid so that every row, column, and 2x3 box contains the letters of the word "editor."

			I	D	
E				T	
R	T				O
	O				
D					T

CRISS CROSS:
SHAKESPEAREAN CHARACTERS

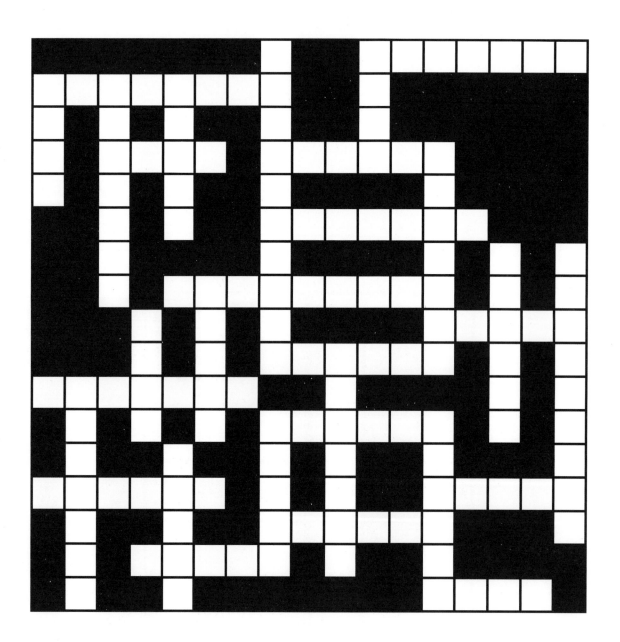

"All the world's a stage" and the characters listed below have graced many. Now though there is a different role for these *dramatis personae* as you find each a place in the grid.

4-letter words
Eros
Hero
Lear
Puck
York

5-letter words
Henry
Lucio
Paris
Percy
Romeo
Timon
Wales

6-letter words
Antony
Caesar
Cicero
Duncan
Edward

Hamlet
Portia

7-letter words
Capulet
Eleanor
Octavia
Ophelia
Richard
Shylock
Warwick

8-letter word
Prospero

9-letter words
Cleopatra
Moonshine

10-letter word
Touchstone

11
LETTER DROP

The letters in each of the columns need to be entered into the squares immediately below, but not necessarily in the same order. By placing the letters in the correct places you will discover a writing tip from Elmore Leonard.

12
WEIRD AND WONDERFUL

Words are a writer's tool and the English language contains many words that are both weird and wonderful. What is the correct meaning of the following?

1 Euonym
a) A name well suited to the person, place, or thing
b) Abbreviated expression, for example: ASAP
c) A favorable review or critique

2 Cheville
a) Witty wordplay
b) To talk gibberish
c) Redundant word or phrase that is used to fill out a verse or sentence

3 Metrophobia
a) Fear of poetry
b) Fear of theatre and live performance
b) Fear of libraries

4 Battology
a) Viking verse
b) Needless repetition of words
c) To use gestures by way of explanation

13

CROSSWORD

Across

9 Stir to action (7)

10 An Ox ion all mixed up (7)

11 Prominent (7)

12 Susan Coolidge revealed what_____? (7)

13 *For Whom the Bell Tolls* author (9)

15 Prufrock poet (5)

16 Smallest (7)

19 Go down (7)

20 Poet Rainer (5)

21 Concealed device (5,4)

25 Ring-shaped (7)

26 Greyhound (7)

28 Warm (7)

29 Ran reel (anag) (7)

Down

1 Oration (6)

2 Rostrum perhaps for 1 down (6)

3 Poet within a soap opera (4)

4 Confer (6)

5 Compete for position (8)

6 Russian novelist (10)

7 Trachea (8)

8 Unrevised book (8)

14 Pen name (3,2,5)

16 Holmes' final problem (8)

17 Not any more (2,6)

18 Progressives (8)

22 English novelist and commentator (6)

23 Rue (6)

24 Cadfael's creator (6)

27 Persia (4)

14

PICTURE POSER

Which novel's title is suggested by the following?

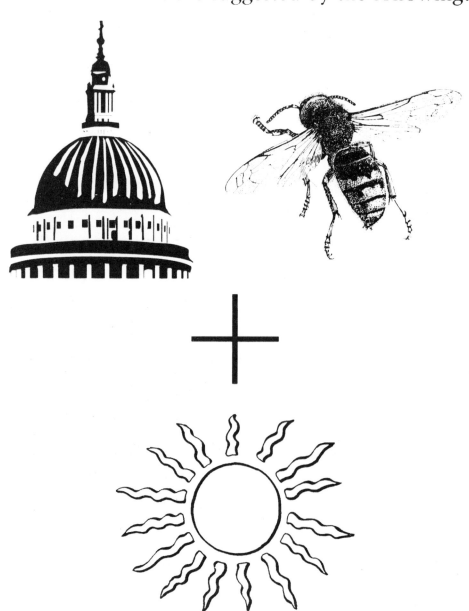

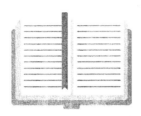

15

BETWEEN THE LINES

A word of immediate interest can be inserted into the blank line so that, reading downwards, nine three-letter words are formed. What is the word hidden between the lines?

A	B	A	L	I	F	S	B	W	M
M	T	E	D	E	R	Y	G	Y	T

16
WORD LADDER

On many a bookshelf lurks a handbook—and there are handbooks on a wide range of subjects. In this word ladder, changing one letter at a time, turn "hand" into "book."

Hand

Book

17
STRANGE BUT TRUE

Thomas Carlyle's three-volume work, *The French Revolution: A History,* was a major and influential work, not only in its vivid portrayal of events in France but with Charles Dickens using it as a major reference for his novel *A Tale of Two Cities.* But what happened to Carlyle's first manuscript?

a) On learning of Thomas Carlyle's research and writing, a French aristocrat hired a robber to steal the manuscript. He was concerned that family secrets and his family's complicity in events were about to be revealed. Bizarrely, after reading the stolen manuscript and finding his fears misplaced, the aristocrat returned the manuscript to Carlyle, giving him additional material to use.

b) A housemaid accidently burned the manuscript, causing Thomas Carlyle to rewrite the first volume again.

c) The young Queen Victoria, who herself had literary ambitions, was so impressed with the style and writing of Carlyle's work she asked to meet the author. Hearing of the Queen's praise, Carlyle presented the Queen with a signed and inscribed copy of the manuscript. This is still kept in the archive at Windsor Castle.

18
WORD QUEST

Make as many words of four or more letters as possible from the nine letters below. In making a word, each letter may be used only once and each word must always contain the central letter, H. Plurals and proper names do not count. A word describing something that features in many a story can be made by using all nine letters.
Scoring: 21 words excellent; 17 very good.

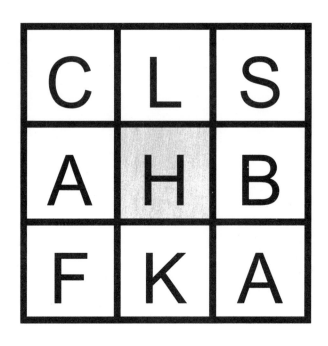

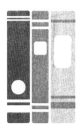

19

A LITERARY RIDDLE

My first is in hope, never in despair
My second is in glance but not in stare
My third is in write as opposed to fight
And my fourth is in delight, not in fright
My fifth is in full rather than empty
And my sixth is in plenty without being in twenty
My seventh is in story and in prose
I am a writer, that I'll disclose
And even though one of my characters you may not see
The shape of things I did once foresee.
Who am I?

20
WORD SEARCH: BEATRIX POTTER

```
T H M P I G L I N G B L A N D S K
E U T R A Q Y X D E E E B M P R C
P N O P E T E R R A B B I T J E O
P C M T C H B T K E N V Y O L K R
O A K Z I F S U D M K N H K Q S B
M M I G I M X I R D N N N Z X I Y
S U T V O D M M F U N I I C W H M
S N T V E X C Y B Y W U X P X W M
I C E Z A G Y N T Y M O S E N L O
M A N P R K I O G I I E T O E E T
T B J E X M W G M F P H R B H U K
Y N G W A N I C Z R J T R E T M W
X O B J M T P T I H T S O S J A U
R M N O S L Y O R Y Y O A E H S C
X E U R K D V Y I S Q H D X S W V
B S M R S T I T T L E M O U S E L
E J E M I M A P U D D L E D U C K
```

Beatrix Potter once famously declared, "Thank goodness I was never sent to school; it would have rubbed off some of the originality." Luckily, her originality gave rise to many memorable and much-loved creations. In this word search, find the following, including Peter Rabbit, safely burrowed between the letters.

Benjamin Bunny	Mrs. Tittlemouse
Hunca Munca	Mr. Tod
Jemima Puddleduck	Peter Rabbit
Jeremy Fisher	Pigling Bland
Johnny Townmouse	Samuel Whiskers
Miss Moppet	Timmy Tiptoes
Mr. McGregor	Tom Kitten
Mrs. Tiggywinkle	Tommy Brock

MYSTERY SUDOKU

Complete the grid so that every row, column, and 3x3 box contains the letters EFHNORSTY in any order. One row or column contains the last name of a well-known thriller writer.

						H	N	E
							O	
	S	E	O			H	R	F
		O				R	Y	
S			Y		E			R
		Y	T			N		
	E	S	H		N	O	R	
	N							
R	H	F						

22

ON TRACK

Starting with the circled letter and moving one letter at a time either horizontally or vertically, find the names of eight best-selling writers.

Ⓖ	R	I	C	O	R	O
N	I	S	M	R	B	W
G	K	H	A	N	N	N
J	L	L	E	W	I	A
A	M	E	T	T	C	B
S	E	H	C	V	M	L
P	R	A	T	I	D	A

CRYPTOGRAM

Solve the cryptogram to discover an observation from
Jean Cocteau. To give you a start,
M = G, T = O, and A = P.

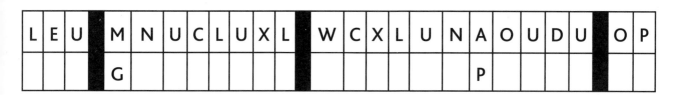

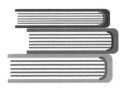

24

A PERPLEXING POSER

Cross out five letters to reveal a popular book.

FAIPVOPELUELARTBTOEORKS

29

25
CRISS CROSS: PUBLICATIONS

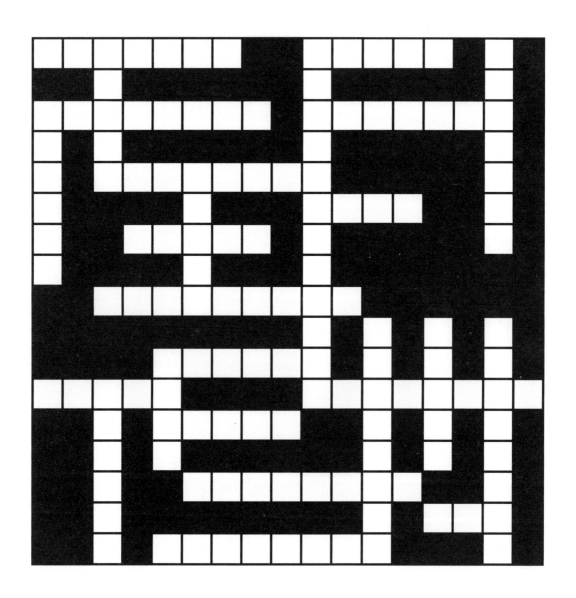

Publications come in many forms and cover all sorts of genres. In this criss cross, fit the following literary mix into the grid.

3-letter word	7-letter words
War	Fiction
	Omnibus
4-letter words	Western
Play	
Saga	**8-letter words**
	Brochure
5-letter words	Chick lit
Atlas	Cookbook
Bible	Handbook
Comic	Pamphlet
Crime	Songbook
Guide	Textbook
Novel	
Sci fi	**9-letter word**
	Adventure
6-letter words	
Poetry	**12-letter word**
Puzzle	Short stories
Volume	

26
ACROSTICS

Solve the clues correctly and the first and last letters will spell a prize-worthy writer.

1 Brigand
2 Spiced sausage
3 Annul
4 Novelist Mr. Bennett
5 Decline

27
WRITERS' TALK

The following are incomplete quotes from Blaise Pascal, Tennessee Williams, and Colleen McCullough. Complete the quotes with each author's exact words.

1 "The last thing one knows when writing a book is what _____."
    a) to call it
    b) to put first
    c) direction it will take

2 "What shouldn't you do if you're a young playwright? _____!"
    a) Let a good review go to your head
    b) Don't bore the audience
    c) Include characters who have no real part

3 "It's a dead give away of an inexperienced writer if every character _____."
    a) speaks with the same voice
    b) exclaims, declares, laughs or shouts
    c) is described in excruciating detail

28
WORD SEARCH: CHILDREN'S WRITERS

```
J T Y L S H N H Y H P R U M E N S
F D U C L E A R Y M P J R U A G J
G S B Y F P D K O A B C J M V P V
P H K T E W R L N O T Y L B V Z Y
R O D J A N S O N N G L M F S I U
B R M C B G W S E N U K S E U S S
W O C R E X F I E P W J N D B S F
C W W O V X L Q E V Y R E T T O P
W I V M U K M D L E A A S X Q N Z
B T B P V Y A S R N N E O U I C E
U Z Y T C H E M A Q G O R S E M G
A U E O L Q T I C I N S S G U E Z
A E Z N H W I T M H I X S L R A K
B K M L U Z H H L W L H B L I A H
W S T I N E W L E H W J K E D W H
F D O K M I N L R O F D N A H W
E N I F K E O C A R R O L L G M B
```

34

Weaving stories of magic, adventure, and fantasy, these writers of books for children have enchanted many a reader. Now is the time to seek out these inventive tellers of tales.

Awdry	Jansson
Blume	Lewis
Blyton	Murphy
Carle	Potter
Carroll	Pullman
Cleary	Rosen
Crompton	Rowling
Dahl	Seuss
Fine	Smith
Handford	Stine
Hargreaves	White
Horowitz	Wilson

MINI SUDOKU: AUTHOR

Canadian novelist Robertson Davies once said, "Authors like cats because they are such quiet, lovable, wise creatures, and cats like authors for the same reasons." I am sure quite a few authors would agree. In this mini sudoku, complete the grid so that every row, column, and 2x3 box contains the letters of the word "author."

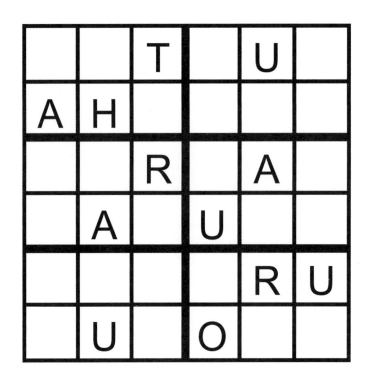

30

WEIRD AND WONDERFUL

What is the correct meaning of the following?

1 Neologism
a) To cite an example
b) Dramatic monologue
c) New word, phrase, or meaning for an existing word

2 Decatessarad
a) Poem of 14 lines
b) Short synopsis
c) Scholarly report

3 Diaskeuast
a) List of bullet points
b) Travelling story teller
c) Someone who edits or revises

4 Squib
a) Pot-boiler
b) Short piece of satirical writing
c) Brief synopsis outlining a plot

31
ANAGRAMS

Time to up the tempo and unscramble the following to discover the names of some American thriller writers.

1 Knot a dozen

2 Hide cell

3 A noble ranch

4 Own brand

5 Thrice shaky

CODED CROSSWORD

Each letter of the alphabet has been replaced by a number. To solve the puzzle, you must decide which letter is represented by which number. To help you start, one word has been partially completed. When you have solved the code, complete the grid at the bottom of the page to reveal what Dorothy Parker considered to be the two most beautiful words in the English language.

17		13		19		21		8		6		16		9
20	3	25	14	22	9	18		24	21	3	11	15	9	16
15		22		18		15		20		24		17		12
16	22	18	2	3	24	4		23	9	18	9	3	23	22
15		21			21		1		16		21		18
17	22	10	20	3	16	22	4	22		9	20	15	9	4
			16			9		20		16		22		
22	5	21	18	9	17	21		12	18	15	2	22	15	16
4		18		20		9			4					
17	1	15	20	20		26	3	20	23	7	24	4	15	17
9		14		26		26		22			22		3	
11	9	18	20	3	24	18		2	22	4	11	22	18	4
15		9		24		9		15		3		4		7
4	9	7	24	18	9	15		21	3 (O)	18 (R)	16	9	12	3
7		4		4		20		10		22		25		4

1	2	3 O	4	5	6	7	8	9	10	11	12	13
14	15	16	17	18 R	19	20	21	22	23	24	25	26

17	1	22	13	24	22		22	16	17	20	3	4	22	12

33
NAME BUILDER

The nine letters of a writer's name have been numbered one to nine. Solve the clues to discover the writer. Can you name two well-known characters that this writer created?

Letters 3, 7, and 6 give us a twosome

Letters 8, 5, 4, and 3 give us a shack, perhaps to get rid of

Letters 4, 1, and 9 give us a female sheep

Letters 8, 5, 2, and 1 give us something that must go on

Letters 5, 6, and 9 give us a garden tool

And letters 2, 3, and 9 give us a lyrical verse.

1	2	3	4	5	6	7	8	9

34
WORKING TITLES

Victor Hugo once considered calling his novel *The Hunchback of Notre-Dame*, "What There Is in a Bottle of Ink." No doubt such a suggestion caused a rethink, but before many titles were decided upon, many famous books had working titles or initial titles suggested by their author. Match the published book title (in the left column) to its working title.

1 *1984*	a) Strangers from Within
2 *To Kill a Mockingbird*	b) Elinor and Marianne
3 *Pride and Prejudice*	c) The Last Man in Europe
4 *War and Peace*	d) Susan
5 *Of Mice and Men*	e) All's Well that Ends Well
6 *The Lord of the Flies*	f) The High-Bouncing Lover
7 *Northanger Abbey*	g) Something that Happened
8 *Sense and Sensibility*	h) Atticus
9 *The Great Gatsby*	i) First Impressions

35

STRANGE BUT TRUE

What was unusual about the German poet
Gottlob Burmann?

a) He always started a new poem on a Monday,
worked on it during the week, and finished it on Friday.
This meant he wrote 52 poems a year—an output he
maintained for more than a decade.

b) He was a wrestler and before each match recited
a poem. This way he could bring his poetry to the
attention of many and, being a good performer, built
up a following. His poetry was more successful than his
wrestling because, in spite of his powerful stature, he
won few contests.

c) He disliked the letter "r" and so excluded it from
all his poems.

36
EXPRESSIVE WORDS

Willard Funk, the son of the well-known author and dictionary publisher, compiled a list of what he considered to be the ten most expressive words in the English language. Match the words to the meaning he ascribed them.

1 The most bitter	a) Tranquil
2 The most tragic	b) Faith
3 The most revered	c) Death
4 The most beautiful	d) No
5 The most cruel	e) Friendship
6 The most peaceful	f) Alone
7 The saddest	g) Mother
8 The warmest	h) Revenge
9 The coldest	i) Love
10 The most comforting	j) Forgotten

WORD LADDER

A rare book can be a prized and sometimes valuable possession. In this word ladder, changing one letter at a time, turn "rare" into "book."

Rare
Book

MYSTERY SUDOKU

Complete the grid so that every row, column, and 3x3 box contains the letters ABCEHMOPT in any order. One row or column contains the seven-letter name of someone well-known in literature. Who is this mysterious figure?

	O	B				A		
		P	O					
		M		A	E		H	
	A							
B	H			M			A	T
							C	
	M		A	T		O		
					C	T		
		T				P	B	

WORD SEARCH:
LORD OF THE RINGS

```
R F T I I A R B E J U Y L N V P Z
P L U L J E Y H E Y S Q Q W S R D
V A Y M F B T R R Q B P P O B I H
P D F I U L N I P P I P A R O D Q
F N J G T S A G A D A R N M R L K
X A F J M E L R O N D I A T O A R
S G Y E M E G O L L U M R O M H I
O A R W C F N J X I A A I N I R P
X R L Y R S B F C J T R O G R K O
Y G L O R F I N D E L A N U C B Z
C D N Z G R R Z Y O L F Q E V S R
Q H B F O E A S O W G D L B I S R
B T U B R E L A N Y N E A S G H L
E R L V O O Y U E N B V J R R E N
Z I L M M C D R W O V B J F I L E
B N E B Z R R O R M E N Y H X O A
A R A G O R N N A J L N J Q C B N
```

The epic fantasy, *The Lord of the Rings*, is one of the best-selling novels ever written, with an estimated 150 million copies sold. Enjoy seeking out some of the wonderful creatures and characters Tolkien created without any need to venture into Middle-earth—or anywhere else for that matter.

Anárion	Gandalf
Aragorn	Gimli
Arwen	Glorfindel
Bilbo	Gollum
Boromir	Haldir
Celeborn	Legolas
Eldarion	Merry
Elrond	Pippin
Éomer	Radagast
Éowyn	Sauron
Faramir	Shelob
Frodo	Wormtongue

40
CRYPTOGRAM

Solve the cryptogram to reveal a short verse written by this author. To give you a start, N = W and P = F.

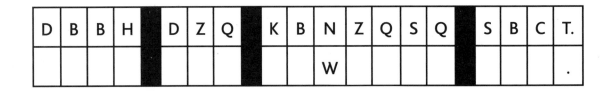

D	B	B	H		D	Z	Q		K	B	N	Z	Q	S	Q		S	B	C	T.
											W									.

V	A	C	T		W		T	W	T.		J	Q	D		K	B	-	B	K	Q,
									.								-			,

O	L	D		W		P	B	L	K	T		J	U	X	Q	A	P.
						F											F.

41
CROSSED WORDS

Solve the clues to reveal in the shaded squares
the name of a best-selling writer.

1 Horse cab
2 Arabian sailor
3 Tree famed for its seeds and wood
4 Plant life
5 Take heed
6 Finally

¹H	A	N	S	O	M
²P	I	R	A	T	E
³C	H	E	R	R	Y
⁴F	L	O	R		
⁵L	I	S	T	E	N
⁶A	T	L	A	S	T

E
R
H
I
M
T
I
E
A
T

42

CRISS CROSS: LITERARY TERMS

There are many forms of literature and ways to use language, including the following. Fit all the words into the grid.

3-letter word	7-letter words
Ode	Epitaph
	Imagery
4-letter words	Tragedy
Epic	
Myth	**8-letter words**
	Quatrain
5-letter words	Syllable
Genre	
Irony	**9-letter word**
Novel	Ambiguity
Prose	
Rhyme	**10-letter words**
Style	Caricature
Theme	Denouement
Verse	Pentameter
	Spoonerism
6-letter words	
Cliche	**12-letter word**
Lament	Alliteration
Satire	
Simile	
Sonnet	

43

WRITERS' TALK

The following are incomplete quotes from Erica Jong, Diane Ackerman, and John Gardner. Complete the quotes with each author's exact words.

1 "The most important thing for a writer is _____."
a) to be locked in a study
b) to have a cast of motley characters
c) to have something to write on, even a cash register receipt or bus ticket will do

2 "One of the real tests of writers, especially poets, is how well they write about _____."
a) loneliness
b) unrequited love
c) smells

3 "A writer's material is _____."
a) what readers want to read
b) spicing up daily life
c) what he cares about

44
MINI SUDOKU: *BEN-HUR*

Lew Wallace's novel *Ben-Hur: A Tale of the Christ* has been hailed as the "most influential Christian book of the nineteenth century" and was the first work of fiction to be blessed by a pope. In this mini sudoku, complete the grid so that every row, column, and 2x3 box contains the letters of the title *Ben-Hur*.

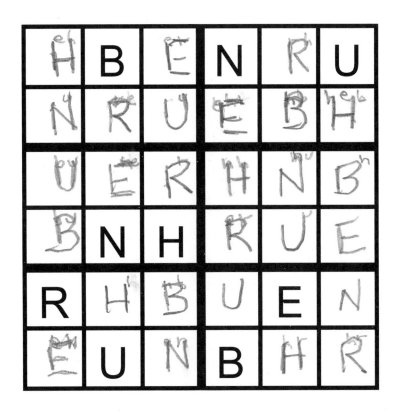

45

WEIRD AND WONDERFUL

What is the correct meaning of the following?

1 Parisology
a) A sentimental poem
b) Use of ambiguous words
c) A musical farce

2 Calligramme
a) Words arranged to create a visual image
b) A sentence, paragraph, or poem in which the words appear in alphabetical sequence, for example: After breakfast, Camilla did eventually fetch great honey in jars . . .
c) A rhyming tongue twister

3 Pleonasm
a) Foreign words that have gained popular usage, for example: au fait
b) To use more words than necessary, for example: burning fire
c) A country saying

4 Lucubrate
a) The overuse of adjectives
b) To emphasise certain text, for instance putting it in **bold** or *italics*
c) To write in a learned manner

46

NOVEL TAKE AWAY

Take away the book title from each of the following seemingly random collection of letters to reveal the book's author.

a) HEMRMOANMBEYLVDILILCEK

b) JMAANNESAFUISELDTPAERKN

c) WIANNAIETHMEPIOLONEH

d) FMRAARNYKESHNESTLELEIYN

e) LOLUIITSATMLEAYWAOLMCOETNT

CODED CROSSWORD

Each letter of the alphabet has been replaced by a number. To solve the puzzle, you must decide which letter is represented by which number. To help you start, one word has been partially completed. When you have solved the code, complete the grid at the bottom of the page to discover what Jean-Paul Sartre considered words to be.

25		2		20		12		6		1		4		9
8	25	13	8	25	18	8		13 A	21	25	1	23	6	13
23		19		1		25		2 S		10		14		1
11	25	13	9	12	11	2		4 H	25	23	14	4	4	12
12		1				2		21		18		14		5
1	25	23	18	2	11	13	11	25		17	24	25	1	16
				11				1		24		13		2
26	23	9	10	23	18	14		25	9	23	14	1	13	21
23		13		10		1				2				
18	12	7	25	10		23	6	25	2	4	25	25	11	2
14		25		3		21		18				7		10
6	13	21	3	23	24	21		22	13	15	10	23	18	25
24		25		1		25		12		23		18		24
9	25	18	13	11	25	2		23	10	10	23	6	23	11
2		11		4		11		18		8		25		4

1	2 S	3	4 H	5	6	7	8	9	10	11	12	13 A
14	15	16	17	18	19	20	21	22	23	24	25	26

| 10 | 12 | 13 | 8 | 25 | 8 | | 9 | 23 | 2 | 11 | 12 | 10 | 2 |

48
FOLLOW THE MUSE

Starting with the circled letter and moving one letter at a time, either horizontally or vertically, find the names of eight poets. Possible a-muse-ment?

D	O	N	F	S	T	L
I	S	N	R	O	N	O
C	K	I	E	F	G	S
W	O	L	L	E	A	T
B	I	N	G	K	S	N
R	N	N	A	O	U	R
O	W	G	E	L	B	U

49
ENTITLEMENT

Each of the following words is missing a letter.
Put the missing letter into the grid below
to reveal the title of a well-known work.
The missing letter from word 1 goes in box
numbered 1, and so on.

1 _REAM

2 STR_P

3 HIKE_

4 A_DER

5 BA_ED

6 B_NDS

7 _AMED

8 FLA_S

1	2	3	4	5	6	7	8

50
NAME BUILDER

The letters of the name of the central figure in several major novels have been numbered one to nine. Solve the clues to discover the identity this mysterious figure. Who wrote the novels?

Letters 3, 2, 6, and 8 give us tender love

Letters 9, 2, 6, and 5 give us a roster

Letters 7, 2, and 1 give us a boar

Letters 4, 2, 9, 5, 1, and 8 involve a search

Letters 3, 5, 4, and 6 give us something ridiculous

While letters 4, 8, 5, and 9 is something this mysterious figure caused.

1	2	3	4	5	6	7	8	9

51

ANAGRAMS: BETWEEN THE COVERS

Unscramble the words to reveal what you will find in many a book.

1 Do indicate

2 Now lacked segment

3 Free cap

4 Arch pet

5 Not scent

52
WORD LADDER

Many an interesting, exciting, or thrilling book has been called a page-turner, and not wanting to be outdone, *The Literary Pocket Puzzle Book* can be heralded as a page-turner through this puzzle. In this word ladder, turn "page" into "turn," preferably without turning to the next page.

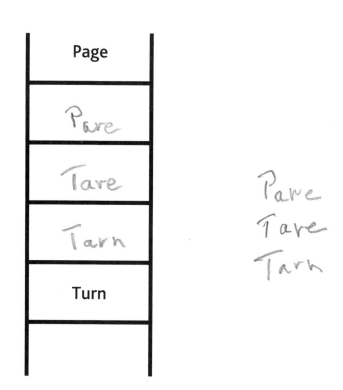

53

WORD SEARCH: ROMANTIC WRITERS

Weaving stories of love, passion and sometimes heartache, all these novelists have touched the hearts and minds of many a reader. Seek them out in what is hopefully a lovely word search.

Austen	Heyer
Beverley	Laurens
Brontë	Mallery
Cartland	McCullough
Chase	McNaught
Cornick	Mitchell
Deveraux	Neels
du Maurier	Plaidy
Fyffe	Quinn
Gabaldon	Roberts
Garwood	Seton
Gaston	Steel

MYSTERY SUDOKU

Complete the grid so that every row, column, and 3x3 box contains the letters BELMOPSTU in any order. One row or column contains a seven-letter word that is an integral part of many a novel.

B	M	L	O	S	U	P		T	E
B	M	L	O	S	U	P	T	E
	O		T	M	E	B	L	S
T	S	E	L					
O	E	M	B	U	L	S	P	T
L	B		E				M	O
	P		M	O		E		L
	U		P	L	O	T	E	
	L		S	E				
E	T		U		M	L	S	P

55

STRANGE BUT TRUE

The French novelist Marcel Proust found himself frequently disturbed by noises outside his apartment. What was his solution?

a) So he could work in absolute silence and be undisturbed, Proust often wrote in the crypt of his local church, sometimes even at night by candlelight.

b) He designed and made a set of special earplugs that excluded outside noise. However, when he developed an ear infection his doctor warned against continuing use of the plugs saying they may cause him to go deaf. Thinking this may even be an advantage Proust carried on wearing them, but did not go deaf.

c) Proust lined his bedroom walls and ceiling with sheets of cork to help reduce outside noise.

56
CRYPTOGRAM

Solve the cryptogram to discover an observation made by the American writer George Ade.
To give you a start, K = Y, R = F, and Z = W.

O	F	L	S	B	D	U	S	K		–		Z	X	H	S		K	F	T		Z	D	U	S	B
P	O	S	T	E	R	I	T	Y		–		W	H	A	T		Y	O	U		W	R	I	T	E

R	F	D		H	R	S	B	D		N	B	U	V	Q		S	T	D	V	B	I		I	F	Z	V
F	O	R		A	F	T	E	R		B	E	I	N	G		T	U	R	N	E	D		D	O	W	N

N	K		O	T	N	Y	U	L	X	B	D	L.
B	Y		P	U	B	L	I	S	H	E	R	S.

57

WEIRD AND WONDERFUL

What is the correct meaning of the following?

1 Palimpsest
a) Re-used page or parchment
b) Political treatise
c) Final proof before printing

2 Lethologica
a) To use long and obscure words
b) Monastic reading room
c) Not remembering the word you want

3 Amphigory
a) Short story with symbolic meaning
b) Sequel, often written by another writer
c) Nonsensical verse

4 Incunabula
a) Pseudonym
b) Book printed before 1501
c) Banned publication

58
A LITERARY RIDDLE

My first is in present as well as in correct
My second is in point but not direct
My third is in leaf but not in tree
My fourth is in spend as well as spree
My fifth is in a lot but never in less
My sixth is in order, thankfully not in mess
My seventh is in yarn as well as in story
Of which I have written many, some quite gory.
Who am I?

59
ACROSTICS

Solve the clues to reveal in the shaded squares the title of a well-known book. Who wrote this book?

1 Cu
2 God of prophecy, poetry, music, and healing
3 Tall dog story
4 Lizard
5 Standard
6 Be against

1 C	O	P	P	E	R
2					
3					
4					
5 N	O	R	M	A	L
6 O	P	P	O	S	E

60

CRISS CROSS: FAMOUS TITLES

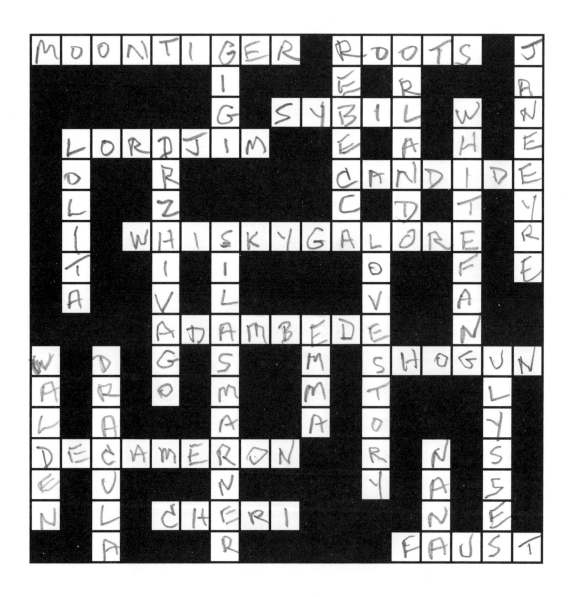

Fit the following famous titles into the grid.

4-letter words

Emma

Gigi

Nana

5-letter words

Chéri

Faust

Roots

Sybil

6-letter words

Lolita

Shogun

Walden

7-letter words

Candide

Dracula

Lord Jim

Orlando

Rebecca

Ulysses

8-letter words

Adam Bede

Jane Eyre

9-letter words

Decameron

Dr Zhivago

Love Story

Moon Tiger

White Fang

11-letter word

Silas Marner

12-letter word

Whisky Galore

PICTURE POSER

Who is suggested by the following?

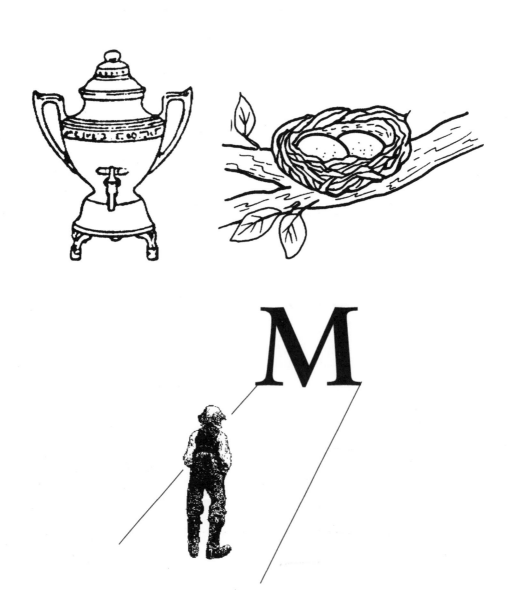

62
LETTER DROP

The letters in each of the columns need to be entered into the squares immediately below but not necessarily in the same order. By placing the letters in the correct places you will discover an interesting Chinese proverb.

63

CODED CROSSWORD

Each letter of the alphabet has been replaced by a number. To solve the puzzle, you must decide which letter is represented by which number. To help you start, one word has been partially completed. When you have solved the code, complete the grid at the bottom of the page to reveal what Henry James considered to "have always been the two most beautiful words in the English language."

23		26		11		23		12		18		7		24
21	7	16	18	21	21	14		15	14	4	9	3	16	25
16		12		16		10		2		1		7		1
15	16	26	20	4	18	2		25	1	22	8	23	1	26
15		14				20		14		9		26		26
16	25	12	4	14	25	12	26	20		12	4	16	10	7
				23				26		16		14		4
4	7	19	7	23	23	1		21	2	1	7	22	1	24
7		15		20		26				22				
7	6	20	16	12		26	21	7	21	14	19	19	16	26
5		7		1		1		8				7		4
13	16	22	7	26	16	23		14	4	15	1	22	9	14
		I	N											
22		14		16		21		9		1		21		12
14	20	26	17	14	26	7		20	22	23	14	20	26	21
26		7		22		9		24		13		4		2

1	2	3	4	5	6	7	8	9	10	11	12	13
14	15	16	17	18	19	20	21	22	23	24	25	26
		I						N				

| 24 | 20 | 25 | 25 | 7 | 4 | | 1 | 5 | 26 | 7 | 4 | 22 | 14 | 14 | 22 |

74

TITLE BUILDER

The letters of the name of a best-selling book, which was also made into a film, have been numbered one to nine. Solve the clues to discover the book's title. Who wrote the book and the screenplay?

Letters 3, 4, 6, and 7 is to forbid

Letters 8, 2, 5, and 9 give us an optimistic color and outlook

Letters 5, 6, 2, 7, and 1 give something to sit upon

Letters 8, 4, 1, and 9 is to depend on

And letters 5, 2, 1, 3, and 4 spell out what you are currently trying to do—and may well have now done!

L	O	V	E	S	T	O	R	Y
1	2	3	4	5	6	7	8	9

65
MINI SUDOKU: AUSTEN

Jane Austen once wrote, "sense will always have attractions for me," but can you make sense of this mini sudoku? Complete the grid so that every row, column, and 2x3 box contains the letters of Jane's last name, "Austen."

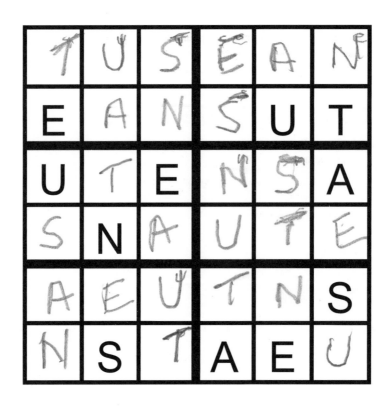

66

WRITERS' TALK

The following are incomplete quotes from Aldous Huxley, E. M. Forster, and Bertrand Russell. Complete the quotes with each author's exact words.

1 "Every man's memory is _____."
  ✓ a) his private literature
  b) a potential story
  c) colored by his reading

2 "One always tends to overpraise a long book, because _____."
  ✓ a) one has got through it
  b) one has made friends with some of its characters
  c) a long book soon becomes a friend

3 "There are two motives for reading a book; one, that you enjoy it; the other, that _____."
  a) it is better than washing the dishes
  ✓ b) you can boast about it
  c) that you may come away wiser

67
TITLE TRACK

Time for a dramatic pause! Starting with the circled letter and moving one letter at a time, either horizontally or vertically, find the titles of six plays written by the Bard of Avon.

Ⓣ	W	E	N	I	T	O
E	B	L	H	G	H	T
L	M	F	T	L	E	H
I	Y	C	O	L	M	A
N	E	K	I	E	T	C
E	L	G	N	L	E	B
A	R	H	A	M	T	H

68
PEN NAMES

In his writings and posturing Benjamin Franklin used a great many names, including Alice Addertongue and Anthony Afterwit. Match the writers' real names (in the left column) to their pen names.

1 Cecil Day-Lewis	a) Edgar Box
2 Samuel Langhorne Clemens	b) George Orwell
3 Gore Vidal	c) Lewis Carroll
4 David Cornwell	d) Paul French
5 Isaac Asimov	e) Robert Markham
6 Eric Arthur Blair	f) Nicholas Blake
7. Stephen King	g) John Wilson
8 Kingsley Amis	h) John le Carré
9 Charles Lutwidge Dodgson	i) Mark Twain
10 Anthony Burgess	j) Richard Bachman

69

WORD SEARCH: HORROR WRITERS

```
N X L Y R M K S U B F I S O C W G
K L U G B Y O H K L B R T T D X Q
D U L E B A O E T Z L C A F X R S
X M D O K F N L O R M O V K H A N
D L A P K W T L G Q E R W C L L Q
M E Q T S B Z E P H J B O S R S L
U Y Q K F U U Y B P X L R Z A P Z
T O S E M A J A D U B L I E H U M
E P Q T E C Y N R O N F H Z H M L
O S L Y P C E O Q T O A B M C P U
R H T K M E Q S V V S W F Z U P P
Y S B I Q H D E N L A Z K E N P T
H E L N N V P H Z P Y V R C L V W
M Y N G U E L T L L E B P M A C N
E C R E I B B A R K E R N F F L R
Y W C T Y X J M B S T O K E R K B
M A S T E R T O N Y R U B D A R B
```

Seek out the last names of these masters and mistresses of horror, if you dare!

Barker	Le Fanu
Bierce	Lumley
Blackwood	Masterton
Bloch	Matheson
Bradbury	Poe
Campbell	Saul
Herbert	Shelley
James	Stine
King	Stoker
Koontz	Straub

70
CROSSWORD

Across

1 Arthur C. _____ (6)
5 German-born British astronomer (8)
9 Flight recorder (5,3)
10 Crystal clear (6)
11 Print composition (10)
12 Consumes (4)
13 Elizabeth Gaskell novel (8)
16 Condescends (6)
17 High-pitched tone (6)
19 Goethe's Apprentice (8)
21 Heroic tale (4)
22 Fleming's precious digit (10)
25 Hitchcock thriller (6)
26 Identifying signal (4,4)
27 George MacDonald Fraser's military cad (8)
28 Scrubs (6)

Down

2 Candy money (5)
3 Right-hand page (5)
4 Trade stoppage (7)
5 Having six feet (7)
6 Passed on (7)
7 Shakespearean tragedy (9)
8 Exit scene (anag)(9)
14 Dry run (9)
15 Annoyances (9)
18 Space behind seats (7)
19 Hi-tech Valley (7)
20 Hornung's cricketer and gentleman thief (7)
23 Harry Hole creator (5)
24 Keen (5)

71
CRYPTOGRAM

Solve the cryptogram to reveal some lines from the poet, Mary Pooley. To give you a start, R = P, Z = K, and H = V.

Line 1: REKQ AEKQOJTW M REJV.
(R = P ... R = P ...)

Line 2: NQLFZ LC MC AEKQ TJLOKQJ.
(Z = K ...)

Line 3: OMHEKQ CPJ UEQNO.
(H = V ...)

72
WORD LADDER

Whether to support a book while you read, keep a page conveniently open, or serve as a stand, a book rest certainly has its uses. In this word ladder, change one letter at a time to turn "book" into "rest," after which you may feel you deserve one!

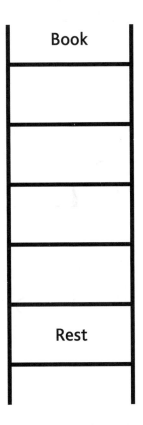

Book

Rest

73

MYSTERY SUDOKU

Complete the grid so that every row, column, and 3x3 box contains the letters ACHIKNPSU in any order. One row or column contains the seven-letter name of a writer. Who is it?

74

STRANGE BUT TRUE

What was the curious habit of Thomas Hardy, the celebrated Dorset writer and poet?

a) Thomas Hardy timed each of his writing sessions by using his prized hourglass. At the end of each session, he allowed himself a break before resetting his glass and working for another hour.

b) He wrote each of his novels with a different pen and then engraved the name of the novel on the pen.

c) Thomas Hardy was fond of drama and sometimes, before going for a walk, dressed in suitable rustic garb. He then proceeded to engage locals in conversation using a thick Dorset accent. This way he was able to learn and understand more about the Dorset dialect that he often incorporated into his novels.

75
ACROSTICS

Solve the clues and the title of a mystery-thriller novel will appear in the shaded squares.

1 Except if

2 Mixed in clue

3 J. K. Rowling's vacancy

4 Nabokov's controversial classic

5 Spinoza's philosophic thoughts

1 U	N	L	E	S	S
2					
3					
4 L	O	L	I	T	A
5					

WORD QUEST

Make as many words of four or more letters as possible from the nine letters below. In making a word, each letter may be used only once and each word must always contain the central letter, O. Proper names do not count. The title of a best-selling book that was later made into a film can be made by using all nine letters.

Scoring: 35 words excellent; 30 words very good.

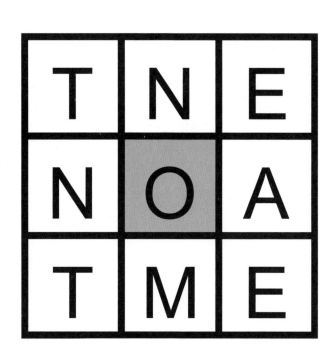

tenon
atone
moat
~~to~~
nonet
atonement
omen
anon
notate

T N E
N O A
T M E

atom
emote
mote
moan
mono
tone
tome
motet
~~m_____no~~
note
tote
neon

77

CODED CROSSWORD

Each letter of the alphabet has been replaced by a number. To solve the puzzle, you must decide which letter is represented by which number. To help you start, one word has been partially completed. When you have solved the code, complete the grid at the bottom of the page to discover what Isaac Bashevis Singer regarded as a writer's best friend.

78
PICTURE POSER

What famous book is suggested by the following?

CRISS CROSS: HARRY POTTER

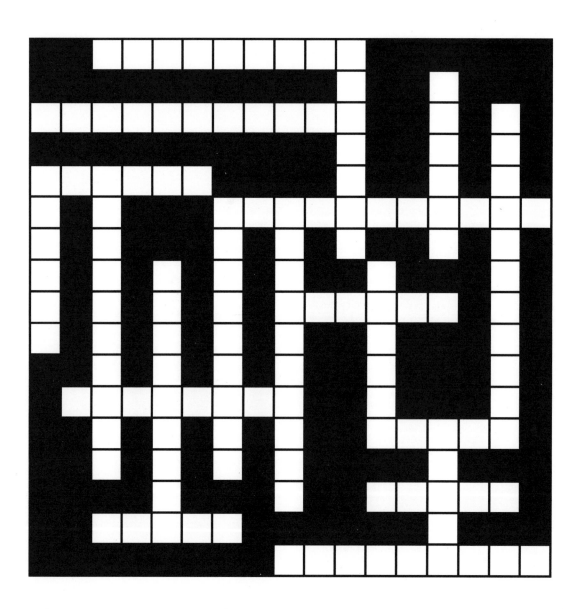

Have a wizard time by fitting the following items and characters from the Harry Potter books, along with the author's name, into the grid.

5-letter words
Broom
Cloak
Dobby
Magic

6-letter words
Hagrid
Hedwig
Howler
Muggle
Wizard

7-letter word
Horcrux

8-letter word
Hogwarts

9-letter words
J. K. Rowling
Quidditch
Slytherin
Voldemort

10-letter words
Dumbledore
Ron Weasley

11-letter words
Draco Malfoy
Harry Potter
Sirius Black

WEIRD AND WONDERFUL

What is the correct meaning of the following words?

1 Peroration
a) A rhetorical question
✓ b) Concluding part of a speech
c) Summary or particularly condensed text

2 Heteronym
a) Shortened word, for example: cafe rather than cafeteria
b) Snappy and apt phrase
✓ c) Word that is written identically to another, but is different in meaning and pronunciation

3 Cacoepy
✓ a) Incorrect pronunciation
b) Prologue
c) Acknowledgements within a book

4 Kabuki
a) Poem in memory of a loved one
b) Verse with each part comprising of a haiku
✓ c) Stylized Japanese drama

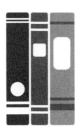

81

BETWEEN THE LINES

The name of an influential poet and philosopher can be inserted into the blank line so that, reading downwards, nine three-letter words are formed. Who is hidden between the lines?

A	C	I	L	O	D	A	A	B
		L		D	ɔ			E
T	T	K	T	E	G	D	E	E

82

PUBLICATION DATE

Put the following publications in the order they were published, from earliest to most recent.

a) *1984* (8)

b) *Little Women* (7)

c) *Jane Eyre* (6)

d) *The Iliad* (1)

e) *The Adventures of Sherlock Holmes*

f) *Romeo and Juliet* (4)

g) *Gulliver's Travels* (5)

h) *The Thorn Birds* (10)

i) *The Da Vinci Code* (11)

j) *Gone With the Wind* (9)

k) *Don Quixote* (3)

l) *The Divine Comedy* (2)

D
L
F
K
G
C
B
E
J
A
H
I

83
A PERPLEXING POSER

As well as penning such classics as *Alice's Adventures in Wonderland* and "Jabberwocky," Lewis Carroll was an accomplished mathematician and also enjoyed inventing and setting puzzles. Here is one he posed:

"Dreaming of apples on a wall,
And dreaming often, dear,
I dreamed that, if I counted all,
—How many would appear?"

How many did appear?

LETTER DROP

The letters in each of the columns need to be entered into the squares immediately below but not necessarily in the same order. By placing the letters in the correct places you will reveal a question that Nora Barnacle Joyce asked her husband James.

		E		D	O	S		
	P	Y		P	L	E		
C	H	U		R	E	A		
W	O	N	O	O	K	N	D	E
Y	A	B	O	W	R	I	T	T
			■				'	
			■					
■	■					■	■	■
■						■	■	■
			■					?

85
MINI SUDOKU: CONRAD

Joseph Conrad once remarked, "But in everything I have written there is always one invariable intention, and that is to capture the reader's attention . . ." With works such as *Lord Jim*, *Heart of Darkness*, and *The Secret Agent* he certainly succeeded and is considered one of the greatest novelists in the English language, even though it was not his native tongue. In this mini sudoku, complete the grid so that every row, column, and 2x3 box contains the letters of the name "Conrad."

WORD SEARCH: JANE AUSTEN CHARACTERS

```
D W R S X E C D T Y T N A R G Y Y
M R M N X B S K E D T E N N E B Q
T F O R C E E L D C D T Q Z R V T
Z U R F L M T R C A P F N J E O H
G U T T W H A X T H S A S B K B D
Q Y O F G A Y V N R L H X Y R Y V
H N N I M E R O L L A Q W E A W J
P A N E B P S C E N L M L O P X I
G K M Q N T O N O J T L V V O O T
S P R M A S E T A B I Y P G C D C
F P F W E X S E S O W C E L V D L
O Y J V O E M N T H O R P E O N U
A M G E W B I R W D A R I A P X T
Y M L R W L U O S A M O R L A N D
R S S N L L E B U R X W K G W T J
K V R O K V M S E C F R O R I L W
V T C N X R N O U Y F A I R F A X
```

In her writing Jane Austen created many memorable characters. Seek out the following persona, which includes some notable heart-throbs.

Allen	Fairfax
Bates	Grant
Bennet	Knightley
Bertram	Morland
Collins	Morton
Crawford	Osborne
Croft	Parker
Darcy	Thorpe
Dashwood	Vernon
Elliot	Watson
Elton	Weston
Emma	Yates

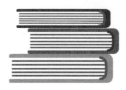

87

ANAGRAMS

Unscramble the anagrams to reveal five well-known book titles.

1 Dual car

2 I danced

3 Am frail man

4 There with gushing

5 Pen ace award

NAME BUILDER

The nine letters of a writer's name have been numbered one to nine. Solve the clues to discover the writer's name.

Letters 5, 4, 3, and 2 give employment

Letters 6, 7, 8, and 2 give us a connection

Letters 9, 3, 4, 5, and 6 give us a snarl

Letters 9, 7, 3, and 6 give us a young woman

And letters 1, 4, 7, and 8 unite.

J	K	R	O	W	L	I	N	G
1	2	3	4	5	6	7	8	9

CRYPTOGRAM

Solve the cryptogram to discover an observation
made by the poet Alexander Pope. To give you a start,
V = U, O = F, and U = K.

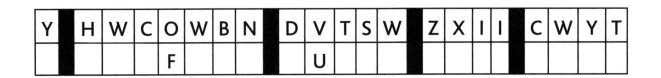

Y | H W C O W B N | D V T S W | Z X I I | C W Y T
(O = F, V = U)

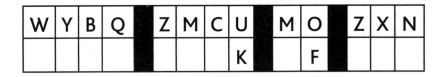

W Y B Q | Z M C U | M O | Z X N
(U = K, O = F)

Z X N Q | N Q W E Y A W | E H X C X N | N Q Y N

X N E | Y V N Q M C | Z C X N.
(V = U)

90
PICTURE POSER

Who is suggested by the following?

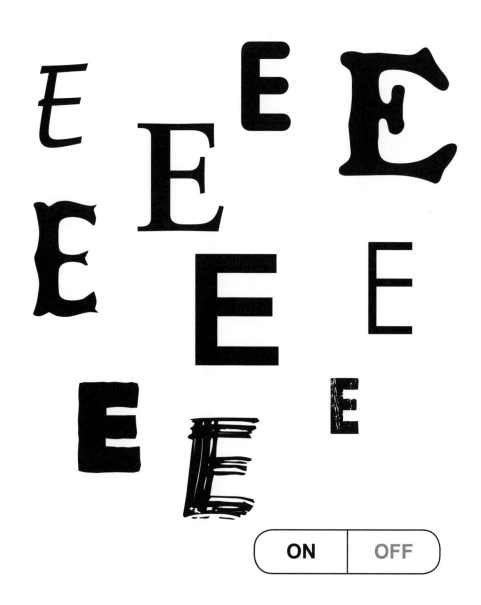

ON | OFF

91
ON TRACK

Starting with the circled letter and moving one letter at a time either horizontally or vertically, find the last names of seven playwrights.

(M)	I	L	A	M	S	C
A	E	L	I	L	E	H
R	P	E	R	L	K	H
E	S	E	W	I	V	O
S	H	K	A	H	S	R
W	A	K	E	P	I	E
B	E	C	T	T	N	T

92
MYSTERY ACROSTIC

During a long career, this writer led many a reader astray with carefully concealed red herrings. In turn, this writer's own name is hidden in two columns of this acrostic. Can you unravel the clues to reveal his or her identity?

1 Hostage money

2 Asian temple

3 Grim harvester

4 Emergency

5 Sufficient

CODED CROSSWORD

Each letter of the alphabet has been replaced by a number. To solve the puzzle, you must decide which letter is represented by which number. To help you start, one word has been partially completed. When you have solved the code, complete the grid at the bottom of the page to discover an item that John Betjeman mischievously added to the collection of London's Geological Museum.

94
MYSTERY SUDOKU

Complete the grid so that every row, column, and 3x3 box contains the letters ADEJMOPSW in any order. One row or column contains the seven-letter name of a writer. Who is it?

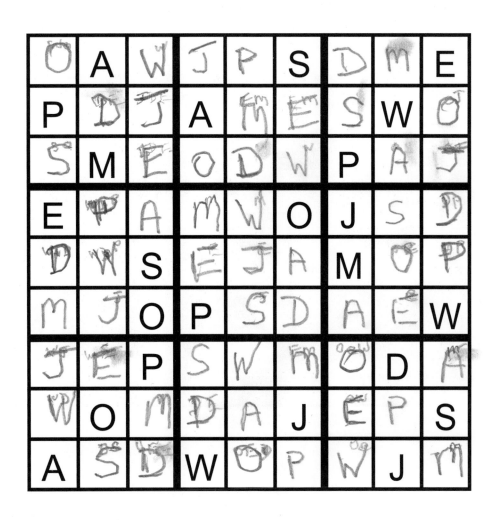

CRISS CROSS:
ROALD DAHL CHARACTERS

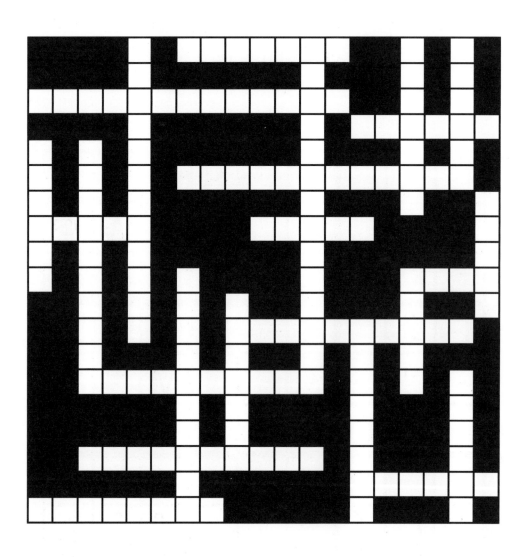

Roald Dahl once declared, "Those who don't believe in magic will never find it." Dahl certainly believed in magic, being able to create many bizarre characters and fantasy worlds. Enjoy some of his creations by fitting each into the grid.

4-letter word
Bean

5-letter words
Billy
Bunce
Danny
James

6-letter words
Boggis
George
Mr. Twit
Sophie
The BFG

7-letter words
Giraffe
Matilda
Mr. Hoppy

8-letter words
Glow-worm
Prodnose

10-letter words
Aunt Spiker
Aunt Sponge
Grandpa Joe
Miss Spider
Willy Wonka

12-letter words
Oompa Loompas
Roly-Poly Bird

13-letter word
Charlie Bucket

14-letter word
Fleshlumpeater

96

A LITERARY RIDDLE

My first is in man but not in kind
My second is in seek, not in find
My third is in threes as well as in fours
My fourth is in lost but not in cause
My fifth is in speak, fortunately not in quarrel
And I always try to convey a timely moral.
Who am I?

WRITE DOWN

Take a letter from the first horizontal row, one from the second and so on until you have formed the seven-letter name of an American writer. Then find the last names of three more American authors. All the letters must be used, but none more than once.

A W T E

H M H N

G E I O

T R R E

L E S M

O A A O

N U U N

98

A PERPLEXING POSER

There are six copies of *The Literary Puzzle Book* on display in an attractive box. Six customers each buy one of the books.

How is it that one copy of *The Literary Puzzle Book* remains in the box?

MINI SUDOKU: PUDNEY

When I was ten, I wrote to the novelist and poet John Pudney and told him that when I grew up I wanted to be a writer. He sent a handwritten letter back saying, "Neil, if you want to be a writer, you have to write, write, and write." And I did. For those with literary aspirations, do bear this advice in mind. This puzzle is dedicated to John Pudney, and in this mini sudoku, complete the grid so that every row, column, and 2x3 box contains the letters of the name "Pudney."

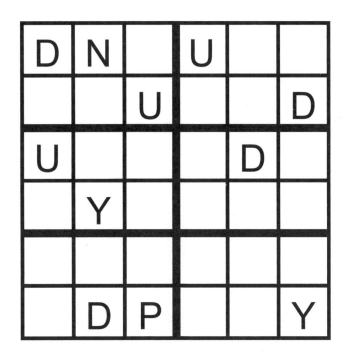

100
PICTURE POSER

What work is suggested by the following?

101
NAME BUILDER

The nine letters of the name of a famous literary character have been numbered one to nine. Solve the clues to discover the identity of this mysterious figure.

Letters 6, 2, 8, 1, and 7 give us a stringed instrument

Letters 9, 7, 5, and 4 give us a portion of medicine

Letters 1, 7, and 6 gives us some work to do

Letters 5, 2, 3, and 4 gives us something identical

While letters 2, 3, 4, 8, and 9 puts right

Which is something that this character does.

1	2	3	4	5	6	7	8	9

WORD SEARCH: SCI-FI WRITERS

```
H H T S B J W H D H C C Q U Y Z E
U Y U K N J C I A B P R R H U A O
V Q G Z G J N I E L N I E H V S Z
C H E B T G F T G W D U B A G N P
E U N S N O M M I S V E L Y J O Q
W X N D Z Q D S B O C E M T H S Y
I L O R R Z W H S K D J R A L N O
Y E V O V B N J O B U D X N N E P
R Y W E L L S J N E A O X J E H A
U N Z H E R B E R T N K I L M P A
B V B T A N G A J S G X L O V E D
D D K E E C V D F T U I J Q M T N
A N R V S S M A D A S Z O S B S I
R Q I D X T C R K O Y P F P V D U
B N H G I G E A N Y B W R R C J G
F A S I M O V R R N O O Q C Z U E
K C I D O Y D K X D E K R A L C L
```

Speculating on times far ahead, of things that may be and sometimes become, science fiction is full of surprise and wonder. Perhaps this word search will cause you to wonder as you seek out the following experts of this genre.

Adams	Heinlein
Asimov	Herbert
Bester	Huxley
Bradbury	Le Guin
Card	Niven
Clarke	Simmons
Dick	Stephenson
Ellison	Verne
Gibson	Vonnegut
Haldeman	Wells

WORD LADDER

Many a reader takes great pleasure as he or she leafs through a book. Hopefully this puzzle may give you equal pleasure as you change one letter at a time and turn "leaf" into "book."

Leaf
Book

104

STRANGE BUT TRUE

How did the English poet Edith Sitwell find her inspiration before starting work?

a) She lay in an open coffin quietly meditating.

b) She threw darts at a dartboard until she hit the bullseye. Then, when she succeeded (or came pretty close) she settled down to write.

c) She made a corn dolly and, due to her expertise, actually wrote a book on the subject, giving instruction on how to make different kinds of dolly and the significance of each.

WRITERS' TALK

The following are incomplete quotes from Charles
Dickens, Stephen King, and Robert Frost. Complete
the quotes with the author's exact words.

1 " . . . there are books of which the _____ are by
far the best parts."
a) illustrations
b) titles
c) backs and covers

2 "I believe the road to hell is paved with _____ . . ."
a) unfinished stories
b) typos
c) adverbs

3 "You can _____ if you come from the right part of
the country."
a) be a little ungrammatical
b) blur fact with fiction
c) have more to write about

106
CRYPTOGRAM

Solve the cryptogram to discover how
Henry David Thoreau said he dealt with insomnia.
To give you a start, I = U, V = L, and M =K.

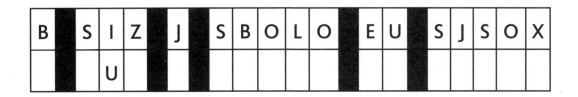

Row 1: B | S I(U) Z | J | S B O L O | E U | S J S O X

Row 2: I(U) Y C O X | A P | S B(L) V(L) V E Q(,) | J Y C | Q R O Y

Row 3: B | L E I(U) V C | Y E Z | G V(L) O O S(,) | B | Q X E Z O

Row 4: B Y | Z R O | C J X M(K).

IT ALL ADDS UP

All the following books have numbers in their titles. When you have the answers, add up all the numbers. The total will suggest the title of a much-loved classic.

a) E. L. James's _____ *Shades of Grey*

b) Joseph Heller's *Catch* _____

c) Nathaniel Hawthorne's *The House of the* _____ *Gables*

d) Dorothy L. Sayers's _____ *Red Herrings*

e) Jerome K. Jerome's _____ *Men in a Boat*

f) Enid Blyton's *Famous* _____

g) Arthur Conan Doyle's *The Sign of the* _____

h) Alexandre Dumas's *The* _____ *Musketeers*

i) J. R. R. Tolkien's *The* _____ *Towers*

MYSTERY SUDOKU

Complete the grid so that every row, column, and 3x3 box contains the letters ADEHLNOUW in any order. One row or column contains the seven-letter name of a writer.
Who is it?

						L	H	N
							W	
	O	N	W		L	D	U	
		W				D	E	
O				E		N			D
		E	A			H		
	N	O	L		H	W	D	
	H							
D	L	U						

109
CRISS CROSS: DICKENS'S CHARACTERS

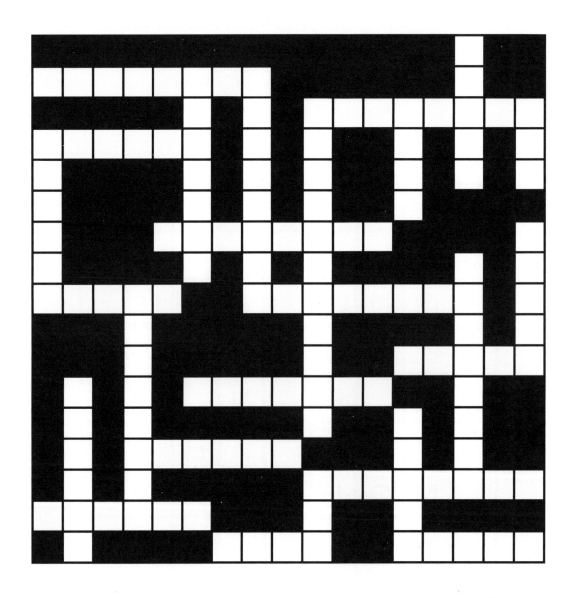

With their quirks and eccentricities Dickens created many memorable—and sometimes ever so 'umble—characters. Fit the following into the grid.

3-letter words
Kit
Pip

4-letter words
Heep
Knag

5-letter words
Betsy
Biddy
Fagin
Nancy
Quilp
Trott

6-letter words
Dorrit
Durden
Feeder
Orlick
Weller

7-letter words
Scrooge
Tiny Tim

8-letter words
Cratchit
Havisham
Magwitch
Micawber
Nicholas
Peggotty
Pickwick
Trotwood

11-letter word
Pumblechook

CROSSED WORDS

Solve the clues to discover in the shaded squares the name of a distinguished writer.

1 Going without clothes
2 Wilde's Mr. Gray
3 Irish writer Edna
4 Famed detective
5 Disclose
6 Crime writer Ian

111

ANAGRAMS

Unscramble the anagrams to discover the names of well-known characters in literature. To help, a clue has been given for each anagram.

1 As wry tome—this young lad certainly enjoyed his adventures

2 Dost warn—something this loyal assistant did on quite a few occasions

3 Restore bow tie—something appropriate for this well-to-do gent

4 Old small fern—the fortunes and misfortunes of a redoubtable woman

5 Treble truth—one of the main protagonists in a classic love story

112
WORD SEARCH: POEMS

```
Z P F B Y S T P E M A V S X Y O A
M U B I O E C N A M O R A P F I J
I L B O H C E W J H M Y R N R X Y
A A K I W A K O Q N K V B A W U S
W G N O S P N B A S O L I T U D E
A L J H A P P I N E S S D B F N G
T L B S T M Y R B E O W U L F D A
D D O P G N M U H B Z W H D L R Y
A K T N T N N O I M Y D N E N E O
L M T A E R E B M E M E R I C A V
X W A K P R X Y F R A N F E X M M
Z C O Q J U M B B A N E R H R S U
Q C V H W X R V D Y D L N K I O Z
B W W A D O N A I S I A V T G S S
C I Z F M C Q G P M A N D A L A Y
D A F F O D I L S V S X J D J U I
O N A I P H R G N I G G I D Y K T
```

Seek out these famous and often influential works.

"Adonais"	"Howl"
"Alone"	"Hudibras"
"Beowulf"	"Mandalay"
"Daddy"	"Ozymandias"
"Daffodils"	"Piano"
"Digging"	"Remember"
"Dreams"	"Romance"
"Echo"	"Solitude"
"Endymion"	"Song"
"Eros"	"Voyages"
"Happiness"	

113
MINI SUDOKU: BRONTË

In the parsonage at Haworth the Brontë sisters wrote some of the classics of English literature, even though some caused much consternation at the time. In this mini sudoku, complete the grid so that every row, column, and 2x3 box contains the letters of the name 'Brontë'.

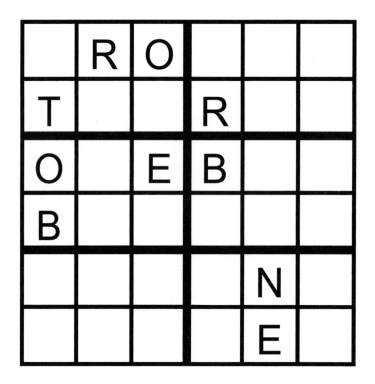

114
PICTURE POSER

What novel is suggested by the following?

ENTRANCE

115
PEN NAMES

Match each female author to her pseudonym.

1 Agatha Christie	a) George Sand
2 Karen Blixen	b) Robert Galbraith
3 Emily Brontë	c) Mary Westmacott
4 Mary Ann Evans	d) Barbara Vine
5 J. K. Rowling	e) Isak Dinesen
6 Doris Lessing	f) George Eliot
7 Louisa May Alcott	g) Jane Somers
8 Amantine-Lucile-Aurore Dupin	h) A. M. Barnard
9 Ruth Rendell	i) Claire Morgan
10 Patricia Highsmith	j) Ellis Bell

116

STRANGE BUT TRUE

How did Walter Scott compose his poem "Marmion?"

a) When fishing on Loch Ness and finding the fish difficult to catch, the poet turned his attention to a much more conducive activity, composing "Marmion."

b) When sitting for a portrait, Walter Scott used the time to compose the poem, dictating his thoughts and lines to the painter who duly recorded them.

c) When riding in the hills near Edinburgh.

117

CLICHES

Writers try to avoid cliches like the plague, but cliches creep into even the best works. In this puzzle, some well-known cliches have had their vowels removed, so perhaps have become "clchs." Can you see the forest for the trees so that the cliches are revealed?

1 THPTCLLNGTHKTTLBLCK

2 PLNTYFFSHNTHS

3 TTHSMMNTNTM

4 DDNSLTTNJRY

5 TTHNDFTHDY

6 FNLYWLLSCLDTLK

118
NAME BUILDER

The nine letters of a writer's name have been numbered one to nine. Solve the clues to discover his or her identity.

Letters 1, 6, 2, and 5 is to steer clear of

Letters 8, 2, 3, and 6 give us something luxuriant

Letters 1, 5, 4, 7, and 9 give us a slow-moving pace

Letters 4, 3, and 6 give us a burnt residue

And letters 5, 7, and 8 leave us with nothing —

Apart from, hopefully, a name.

1	2	3	4	5	6	7	8	9

119

A LITERARY RIDDLE

My first is in major but not in part

My second is in broken, not in heart

My third is in real, never in fake

My fourth is found in a river, not in a lake

My fifth is seen in a star but not in the sky

My sixth is in where, never in why

My seventh is in short as well as in story

My eighth is resplendent in glory, not in furor

Through dastardly deeds I achieved my fame

But do you yet know my name?

FINAL TRACK

Starting with the circled letter and moving horizontally, vertically, or diagonally one square at a time, discover the title of a well-known work.

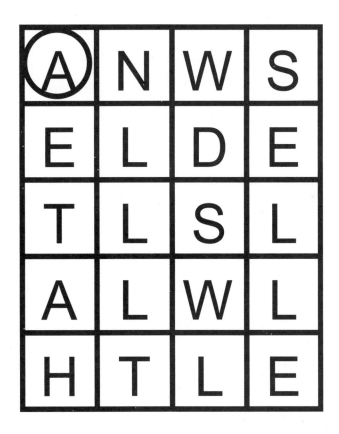

ANSWERS

1 ANAGRAMS: DETECTIVE WRITERS

1 Arthur Conan Doyle, 2 Georges Simenon, 3 Raymond Chandler, 4 James Patterson, 5 Agatha Christie

2 MYSTERY SUDOKU

O	G	E	T	N	L	U	I	K
U	L	T	E	K	I	O	N	G
K	N	I	U	O	G	L	T	E
L	K	O	G	T	U	I	E	N
I	U	G	O	E	N	T	K	L
E	T	N	I	L	K	G	U	O
G	I	K	N	U	O	E	L	T
N	E	U	L	G	T	K	O	I
T	O	L	K	I	E	N	G	U

3 WORD SEARCH: POETS

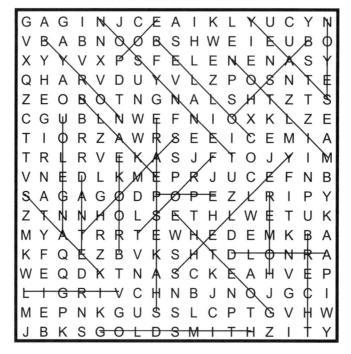

4 WRITERS' TALK
1b, 2c, 3a

5 CRYPTOGRAM
"The best time for planning a book is while you're doing the dishes." Agatha Christie

6 ENTITLED
The Hobbit and the main character is Bilbo Baggins.

7 CODED CROSSWORD

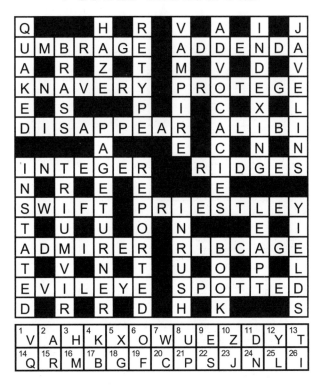

The name in the grid is Alexander Selkirk, who was the inspiration behind Daniel Defoe's *Robinson Crusoe*.

8 CROSSED WORDS
1 Grotto, 2 Secure, 3 Trowel, 4 Emerge, 5 Pledge, 6 Locate
The name in the shaded squares is George Orwell.

9 MINI SUDOKU: EDITOR

O	R	T	I	D	E
E	D	I	O	T	R
I	E	O	T	R	D
R	T	D	E	I	O
T	O	R	D	E	I
D	I	E	R	O	T

10 CRISS CROSS: SHAKESPEAREAN CHARACTERS

11 LETTER DROP

"I try to leave out the parts that people skip."

12 WEIRD AND WONDERFUL

1a, 2c, 3a, 4b

13 CROSSWORD

Across: 9 Provoke, 10 Oxonian, 11 Eminent, 12 Katy did, 13 Hemingway, 15 Eliot, 16 Minimal, 19 Descend, 20 Rilke, 21 Booby trap, 25 Annular, 26 Whippet, 28 Thermal, 29 Learner

Down: 1 Speech, 2 Podium, 3 Pope, 4 Bestow, 5 Jockeyed, 6 Dostoevsky, 7 Windpipe, 8 Unedited, 14 Nom de plume, 16 Moriarty, 17 No longer, 18 Liberals, 22 Orwell, 23 Repent, 24 Peters, 27 Iran

14 PICTURE POSER

Dombey and Son (dome, bee, and, sun)

15 BETWEEN THE LINES

Literature

16 WORD LADDER

One possible solution is: HAND, hank, honk, hook, BOOK

17 STRANGE BUT TRUE

b) Thomas Carlyle lent the manuscript to his friend John Stuart Mill. Unfortunately Mill's maid wrongly thought it was waste paper and burnt it. There was no alternative—Thomas Carlyle had to rewrite the work.

18 WORD QUEST

Abash, backlash, bash, blah, blash, calash, casbah, cash, chal, chalk, clash, fash, flash, **flashback**, haaf, hack, haka, half, halfback, hask, kasbah, lakh, lash, shack

19 A LITERARY RIDDLE

H. G. Wells, author of *The Invisible Man* and *The Shape of Things to Come*.

20 WORD SEARCH: BEATRIX POTTER

```
T H M P I G L I N G B L A N D S K
E U T R A Q Y X D E E E B M P R C
P N O P E T E R R A B B I T J E O
P C M T C H B T K E N V Y O L K R
O A K Z I F S U D M K N H K Q S B
M M I G I M X I R D N N N Z X J Y
S U T V O D M M F U N I I C W H M
S N T V E X C Y B X W U X P X W M
I C E Z A G Y N T Y M O S E N L O
M A N P R K I O G I I E T O E E T
T B J E X M W G M F P H R B H U K
Y N G W A N I C Z R J T R E T M W
X O B J M T P T I H T S O S J A U
R M N O S L Y O R Y Y O A E H S C
X E U R K D V Y I S Q H D X S W V
B S M R S T I T T L E M O U S E L
E J E M I M A P U D D L E D U C K
```

21 MYSTERY SUDOKU

F	O	R	S	Y	T	H	N	E
N	Y	H	R	E	F	S	O	T
T	S	E	O	N	H	R	F	Y
E	F	O	N	H	R	Y	T	S
S	T	N	Y	O	E	F	H	R
H	R	Y	T	F	S	N	E	O
Y	E	S	H	T	N	O	R	F
O	N	T	F	R	Y	E	S	H
R	H	F	E	S	O	T	Y	N

The thriller writer is Frederick Forsyth.

22 ON TRACK
Grisham, Cornwell, King, James, Pratchett, Vidal, McBain, Brown

23 CRYPTOGRAM
"The greatest masterpiece in literature is only a dictionary out of order."

24 A PERPLEXING POSER
If you remove "five letters," you are left with "a popular book." This poser was inspired by the mathematician and prolific author Martin Gardner.

25 CRISS CROSS: PUBLICATIONS

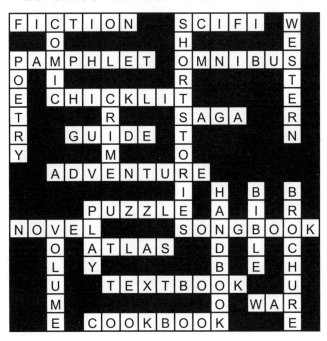

26 ACROSTICS
1 Outlaw, 2 Salami, 3 Cancel, 4 Arnold, 5 Refuse
The first and last columns spell: Oscar Wilde.

27 WRITERS' TALK

1b, 2b, 3a

28 WORD SEARCH: CHILDREN'S WRITERS

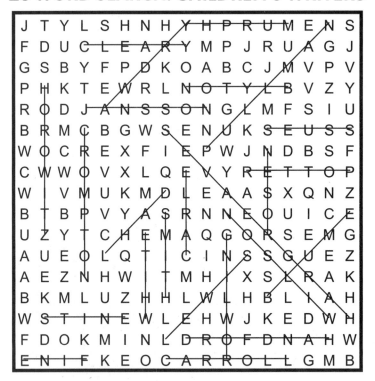

29 MINI SUDOKU: AUTHOR

O	R	T	H	U	A
A	H	U	R	T	O
U	O	R	T	A	H
T	A	H	U	O	R
H	T	O	A	R	U
R	U	A	O	H	T

30 WEIRD AND WONDERFUL

1c, 2a, 3c, 4b

31 ANAGRAMS

1 Dean Koontz, 2 Lee Child, 3 Harlan Coben, 4 Dan Brown,
5 Kathy Reichs

32 CODED CROSSWORD

Dorothy Parker considered the two most beautiful words in the English Language to be: Cheque enclosed.

33 NAME BUILDER

The author is P. G. Wodehouse, and his two most famous creations are Bertie Wooster and his butler/valet, Jeeves.

34 WORKING TITLES

1c, 2h, 3i, 4e, 5g, 6a, 7d, 8b, 9f

35 STRANGE BUT TRUE

c) Gottlob Burmann so disliked the letter "r" that he even avoided using it in his daily speech, which also precluded him from saying his last name!

36 EXPRESSIVE WORDS

1f, 2c, 3g, 4i, 5h, 6a, 7j, 8e, 9d, 10b

This was how Willard Funk classified the words, but with the words subject to individual interpretation, there are really no right or wrong answers. I am sure Willard Funk would have agreed, or I hope so anyway!

37 WORD LADDER

One possible solution: RARE, race, rack, rock, lock, look, BOOK

38 MYSTERY SUDOKU

H	O	B	T	C	M	A	P	E
A	E	P	O	B	H	C	T	M
C	T	M	P	A	E	B	H	O
M	A	C	B	E	T	H	O	P
B	H	O	C	M	P	E	A	T
T	P	E	H	O	A	M	C	B
P	M	H	A	T	B	O	E	C
O	B	A	E	P	C	T	M	H
E	C	T	M	H	O	P	B	A

39 WORD SEARCH: *LORD OF THE RINGS*

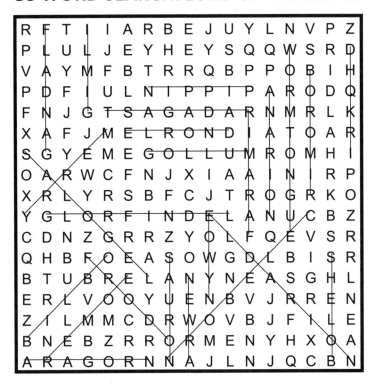

```
R F T I I A R B E J U Y L N V P Z
P L U L J E Y H E Y S Q Q W S R D
V A Y M F B T R R Q B P P O B I H
P D F I U L N I P P I P A R O D Q
F N J G T S A G A D A R N M R L K
X A F J M E L R O N D I A T O A R
S G Y E M E G O L L U M R O M H I
O A R W C F N J X I A A I N I R P
X R L Y R S B F C J T R O G R K O
Y G L O R F I N D E L A N U C B Z
C D N Z G R R Z Y O L F Q E V S R
Q H B R O E A S O W G D L B I S R
B T U B R E L A N Y N E A S G H L
E R L V O Q Y U E N B V J R R E N
Z I L M M C D R W O V B J F I L E
B N E B Z R R O R M E N Y H X O A
A R A G O R N N A J L N J Q C B N
```

40 CRYPTOGRAM

"Took the nowhere road. Glad I did. Met no-one, but I found myself."

41 CROSSED WORD

1 Hansom, 2 Sinbad, 3 Walnut, 4 Botany, 5 Beware, 6 Lastly
The name in the shaded squares is that of award-winning novelist
Hilary Mantel.

42 CRISS CROSS: LITERARY TERMS

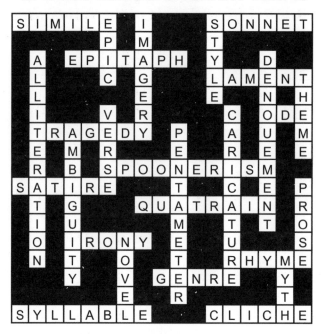

43 WRITERS' TALK

1a, 2c, 3c

44 MINI SUDOKU: *BEN-HUR*

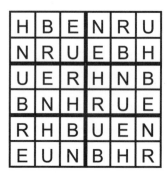

45 WEIRD AND WONDERFUL

1b, 2a, 3b, 4c

46 NOVEL TAKE AWAY

Herman Melville *Moby-Dick*, Jane Austen *Mansfield Park*, A. A. Milne *Winnie the Pooh*, Mary Shelley *Frankenstein*, Louisa May Alcott *Little Women*

47 CODED CROSSWORD

Jean-Paul Sartre once declared words as being "loaded pistols."

48 FOLLOW THE MUSE

Dickinson, Frost, Longfellow, Browning, Angelou, Burns, Keats

49 ENTITLEMENT

Birdsong

50 NAME BUILDER

The central figure was the Godfather. Mario Puzo wrote the novels.

51 ANAGRAMS: BETWEEN THE COVERS

1 Dedication, 2 Acknowledgements, 3 Preface, 4 Chapter, 5 Contents

52 WORD LADDER

One possible solution: PAGE, pare, tare, tarn, TURN

53 WORD SEARCH: ROMANTIC WRITERS

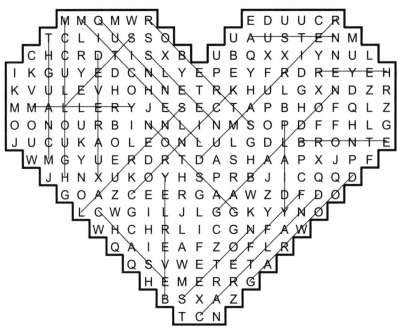

54 MYSTERY SUDOKU

B	M	L	O	S	U	P	T	E
P	O	U	T	M	E	B	L	S
T	S	E	L	P	B	M	O	U
O	E	M	B	U	L	S	P	T
L	B	S	E	T	P	U	M	O
U	P	T	M	O	S	E	B	L
S	U	B	P	L	O	T	E	M
M	L	P	S	E	T	O	U	B
E	T	O	U	B	M	L	S	P

55 STRANGE BUT TRUE

c) In addition to insulating his room from noise, Proust also considered that cork would absorb harmful dust, something he was keen to do as he was asthmatic.

56 CRYPTOGRAM

"Posterity—what you write for after being turned down by publishers."

57 WEIRD AND WONDERFUL

1a, 2c, 3c, 4b

58 A LITERARY RIDDLE

Tolstoy

59 ACROSTICS

1 Copper, 2 Apollo, 3 Shaggy, 4 Iguana, 5 Normal, 6 Oppose
The first and last columns spell *Casino Royale*. This was the first James
Bond novel written by Ian Fleming.

60 CRISS CROSS: FAMOUS TITLES

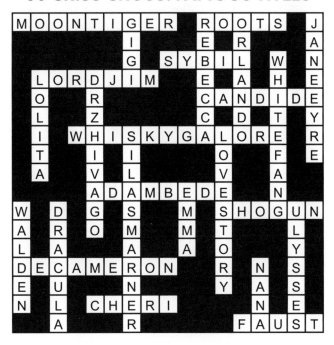

61 PICTURE POSER

Ernest Hemingway (urn, nest, M in way)

62 LETTER DROP

A book is like a garden carried in your pocket.

63 CODED CROSSWORD

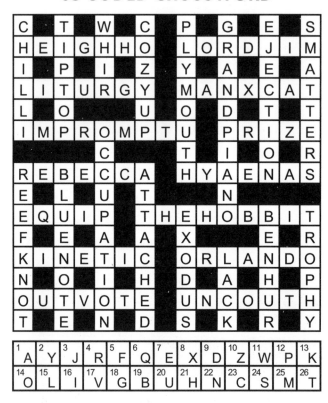

Henry James considered "summer afternoon" to be the two most beautiful words in the English language.

64 TITLE BUILDER

Love Story, which was written by Erich Segal.

65 MINI SUDOKU: AUSTEN

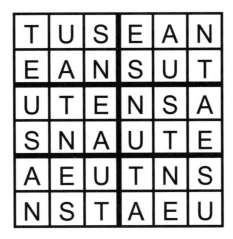

T	U	S	E	A	N
E	A	N	S	U	T
U	T	E	N	S	A
S	N	A	U	T	E
A	E	U	T	N	S
N	S	T	A	E	U

66 WRITERS' TALK
1a, 2a, 3b

67 TITLE TRACK
Twelfth Night, Othello, Cymbeline, King Lear, Hamlet, Macbeth

68 PEN NAMES
1f, 2i, 3a, 4h, 5d, 6b, 7j, 8e, 9c, 10g

69 WORD SEARCH: HORROR WRITERS

70 CROSSWORD

Across: 1 Clarke, 5 Herschel, 9 Black box, 10 Limpid, 11 Typography, 12 Eats, 13 *Cranford*, 16 Deigns, 17 Shrill, 19 Sorcerer, 21 Saga, 22 *Goldfinger*, 25 *Psycho*, 26 Call sign, 27 Flashman, 28 Scours

Down: 2 Lolly, 3 Recto, 4 Embargo, 5 Hexapod, 6 Relayed, 7 *Cymbeline*, 8 Existence, 14 Rehearsal, 15 Nuisances, 18 Legroom, 19 Silicon, 20 Raffles, 23 Nesbø, 24 Eager

71 CRYPTOGRAM
"Pour yourself a poem.
Drink it at your leisure.
Savour the words."

72 WORD LADDER

One possible solution: BOOK, boot, boat, beat, best, REST

73 MYSTERY SUDOKU

I	A	P	S	C	N	K	H	U
N	H	U	A	I	K	C	S	P
K	C	S	U	H	P	A	I	N
U	N	H	K	S	I	P	C	A
C	S	K	P	U	A	H	N	I
A	P	I	C	N	H	S	U	K
P	I	N	H	A	S	U	K	C
H	U	A	N	K	C	I	P	S
S	K	C	I	P	U	N	A	H

74 STRANGE BUT TRUE

b) Thomas Hardy used dip pens—some of which are currently on display at the Dorset County Museum—with the name of the novel written with each pen engraved on its bone handle.

75 ACROSTICS

1 Unless, 2 Nuclei, 3 Casual, 4 *Lolita*, 5 *Ethics*
The first and last columns spelling *Uncle Silas*, the novel by J. Sheridan Le Fanu.

76 WORD QUEST

Aeon, anemone, anno, anon, atom, atone, atonement, emote, eoan, manto, moan, moat, mona, montane, montant, monte, mote, motet, mott, motte, neon, nome, nomen, none, nonet, nonette, notate, note, nott, oaten, omen, omenta, tenon, toman, tome, tonant, tone, tonne, tote, totem

Atonement is a best-selling novel by Ian McEwan.

77 CODED CROSSWORD

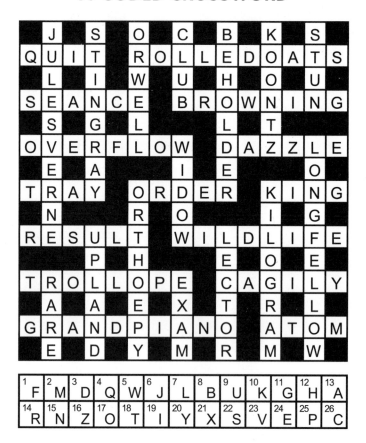

Isaac Bashevis Singer regarded the wastepaper basket as a writer's best friend.

78 PICTURE POSER

The Catcher in the Rye (cat, chair, in the rye)

79 CRISS CROSS: HARRY POTTER

80 WEIRD AND WONDERFUL
1b, 2c, 3a, 4c

81 BETWEEN THE LINES
Coleridge

82 PUBLICATION DATE
d, l, f, k, g, c, b, e j, a, h, i

83 A PERPLEXING POSER
Ten. The clue being "dreaming of *ten*, dear . . ."

84 LETTER DROP
"Why don't you write books people can read?"

85 MINI SUDOKU: CONRAD

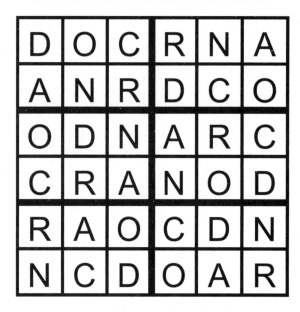

D	O	C	R	N	A
A	N	R	D	C	O
O	D	N	A	R	C
C	R	A	N	O	D
R	A	O	C	D	N
N	C	D	O	A	R

86 WORD SEARCH: JANE AUSTEN CHARACTERS

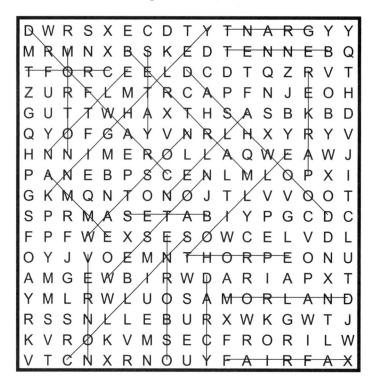

87 ANAGRAMS

1 *Dracula*, 2 *Candide*, 3 *Animal Farm*, 4 *Wuthering Heights*, 5 *War and Peace*

88 NAME BUILDER

J. K. Rowling

89 CRYTPOGRAM

"A perfect Judge will read each Work of Wit
With the same Spirit that its Author writ . . ."

90 PICTURE POSER

Tennyson (ten Es, ON)

91 ON TRACK

Miller, Williams, Chekhov, Shakespeare, Shaw, Beckett, Pinter

92 MYSTERY ACROSTIC

Across: 1 Ransom, 2 Pagoda, 3 Reaper, 4 Crisis, 5 Enough
The name hidden in the third and sixth columns is that of the New Zealand detective writer Ngaio Marsh.

93 CODED CROSSWORD

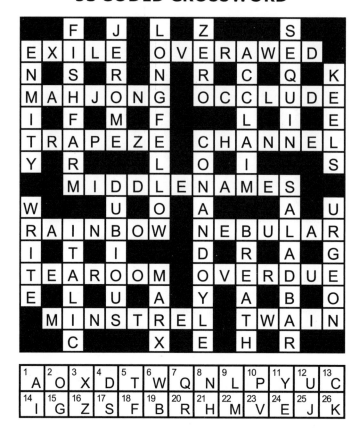

The item that John Betjeman added to the collection was a horse chestnut. He placed it in an unlocked showcase with a suitably inscribed card stating it had been "Donated by J. Betjeman Esquire." It remained part of the collection for some considerable time.

94 MYSTERY SUDOKU

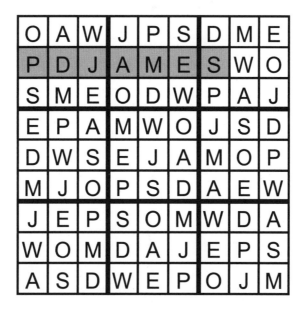

95 CRISS CROSS: ROALD DAHL CHARACTERS

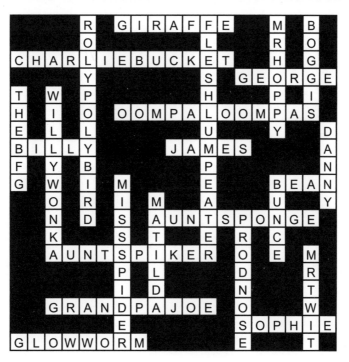

96 A LITERARY RIDDLE
Aesop

97 WRITE DOWN
Angelou, Whitman, Emerson, Thoreau

98 A PERPLEXING POSER
The sixth customer takes the box with the book still inside.

99 MINI SUDOKU: PUDNEY

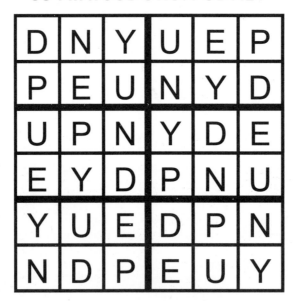

100 PICTURE POSER
Pygmalion (pig, mail, lion)

101 NAME BUILDER
James Bond

102 WORD SEARCH: SCI-FI WRITERS

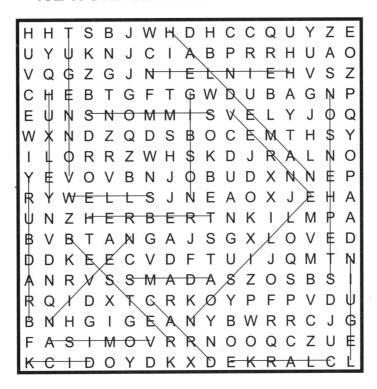

103 WORD LADDER

One possible solution: LEAF, lean, bean, beat, boat, boot, BOOK

104 STRANGE BUT TRUE

a) Edith Sitwell was certainly an eccentric and during her lifetime was particularly known for her unusual dress, which included wearing gold turbans and many rings. Her habit of lying in a coffin is recounted in Diane Ackerman's *A Natural History of the Senses*.

105 WRITERS' TALK

1c, 2c, 3a

106 CRYPTOGRAM

"I put a piece of paper under my pillow, and when I could not sleep, I wrote in the dark."

107 IT ALL ADDS UP

a) Fifty, b) 22, c) Seven, d) Five, e) Three, f) Five, g) Four, h) Three, i) Two
The total of these numbers is 101, suggesting *The Hundred and One Dalmatians* by Dodie Smith.

108 MYSTERY SUDOKU

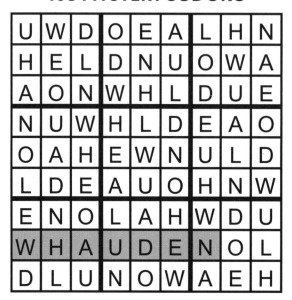

U	W	D	O	E	A	L	H	N
H	E	L	D	N	U	O	W	A
A	O	N	W	H	L	D	U	E
N	U	W	H	L	D	E	A	O
O	A	H	E	W	N	U	L	D
L	D	E	A	U	O	H	N	W
E	N	O	L	A	H	W	D	U
W	H	A	U	D	E	N	O	L
D	L	U	N	O	W	A	E	H

109 CRISS CROSS: DICKENS'S CHARACTERS

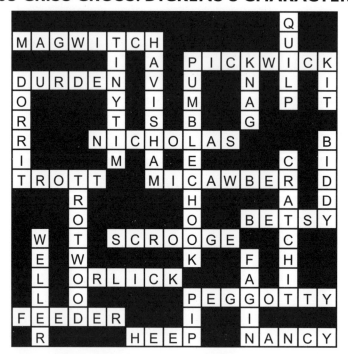

110 CROSSED WORDS

1 Nudism, 2 Dorian, 3 O'Brien, 4 Holmes, 5 Reveal, 6 Rankin
The name in the shaded squares is Norman Mailer, a famous American author and twice winner of the Pulitzer Prize.

111 ANAGRAMS

1 Tom Sawyer, 2 Dr Watson, 3 Bertie Wooster, 4 Moll Flanders, 5 Rhett Butler

112 WORD SEARCH: POEMS

113 MINI SUDOKU: BRONTË

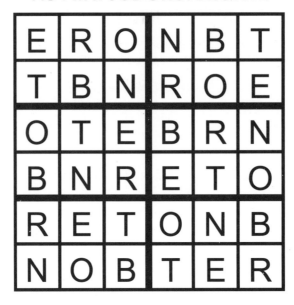

E	R	O	N	B	T
T	B	N	R	O	E
O	T	E	B	R	N
B	N	R	E	T	O
R	E	T	O	N	B
N	O	B	T	E	R

114 PICTURE POSER

Captain Corelli's Mandolin (cap, ten, core, L, Es, man, doll, in)

115 PEN NAMES

1c, 2e, 3j, 4f, 5b, 6g, 7h, 8a, 9d, 10i

116 STRANGE BUT TRUE

c) Walter Scott later told his son-in-law, "Oh, man, I had many a grand gallop among these braes when I was thinking of 'Marmion'."

117 CLICHES

1 The pot calling the kettle black, 2 Plenty of fish in the sea, 3 At this moment in time, 4 Add insult to injury, 5 At the end of the day, 6 If only walls could talk

118 NAME BUILDER

Susan Hill

119 A LITERARY RIDDLE
Moriarty

120 FINAL TRACK
All's Well that Ends Well

ACKNOWLEDGEMENTS

With my love of books and enjoyment of puzzles, this book has been a joy to compile—and I hope a joy that will have brought you and many others pleasure.

In this work I have, as always, been helped by my family, Ros, Richard, and Emily. I am also grateful for the willingness of Barbara Smith and David Finnerty to gamely try some of the puzzles and offer valuable feedback. Gill Richards and Beth Elliot were also able to provide useful information for which I was grateful.

My editor at Summersdale, Stephen Brownlee, backed by his excellent team, have also given wonderful input as well as designing this book in such a splendid way. I am also very grateful to Lyn Coutts for her assiduous checking and helpfulness.

To you all, thank you, and to the reader, I hope you have enjoyed tackling and solving the puzzles within.

Neil Somerville